£5·50

Medieval Islam

PAULA BARTLEY
AND HILARY BOURDILLON

Hodder & Stoughton
LONDON SYDNEY AUCKLAND

ACKNOWLEDGEMENTS

The Publishers would like to thank the following for permission to reproduce illustrations in this volume:
Cover-Vienna Österreichisches Nationalbibliothek, Book of Antidotes (Kitabad Diryaq) of Pseudo-Galen. Scenes from The Royal Court Ms. 134-C AF Fol I Recto; p. 13. Sonia Halliday p. 5 top; p. 23 left; p. 41; p. 43 lower. La Bibliothèque Nationale, Paris Ms Arabe 5847 f. 294v, p. 5; Ms Arabe 5847 p. 8 right; Ms Arabe 5847 f. 19 recto p. 10 right; Ms Arabe 2964 p. 19; Ms Arabe 5847 p. 23 right; p. 28; Ms Arabe 5847 f. 33 p. 31 right; p. 40 right; p. 46; Ms Arabe 5847 p. 47; Ms 5594 f. 9 p. 54 right; Ms Fr. 9084 f. 42 v p. 53.
Reproduced by permission of The British Library, Oriental and India Office Collections Add 16561 f. 60 r p. 26 left; Or 3299 f. 89 recto detail p. 30; Ms Or 2884 f. 17b p. 32; Charta Rogeriana Weltkarte des Idrisi 1154 p. 43 top; Or 2265 f. 66v p. 48 left; Or 3299 f. 291 r. p. 48 right; Or 3299 f. 260 v p. 49; Ms Or 2838 F. 20 v. p. 59 left; Ms Or 6810 f. 154v p. 59 right.
Reproduced by permission of The British Library, Department of Western Manuscripts Ms Egerton 1500 f. 45 v p. 56.
Camerapix p. 6 left; p. 11.
E. T. Archive p. 6 right.
The New York Public Library, Spencer Collection Ms 3 Siyar-e Nabi Fol 343v p. 7.
The J Allan Cash Photolibrary p. 8 left.
Peter Saunders Photography p. 10 left.
Michael Holford p. 14 right.
Amplicaciones Reproducciones MAS p. 15; p. 16.
Patrimonio Nacional Madrid Escorial, Cantigas de Santa Maria f. 181 p. 17.

Topkapi Sarayi Müsezi Müdürlügü Ms H. 841 f. 3 verso p. 20; Ms A2127 F. 2 verso p. 35 left.
Clare Weaver p. 21.
Istanbul University Library T. 5964 F. 105r. p. 25.
Reproduced by Permission of the Board of Trustees of the Victoria and Albert Museum, London p. 29.
Werner Forman Archive p. 33.
Wellcome Institute Library, London p. 35 right.
Millet Library, Istanbul Ms T. 79 p. 36.
Edinburgh University Library OR Ms. 161 F. 16 r p. 37; OR Ms 161 Fol 134v p. 53 right; OR Ms 20 f. 52r p. 62 lower.
The Ann Ronan Picture Library p. 38 both.
Biblioteca Universitaria di Bologna Ms. Avicenna 2197 f. 492 p. 39 right.
Reproduced by permission of The Metropolitan Museum of Art Ms 55.121.11 reverse, Syrian, 1315. Design for a water raising device from an *Automata* by Abu'l Izz Isma'il al Jazari p. 42.
Reproduced by courtesy of the Trustees of the British Museum p. 45 lower left.
Österreichische Museum für Angewandte Kunst, Portuguese Carpet 17 JH. (Inv T8339) p. 45 right.
Ronald Sheridan/The Ancient Art and Architecture Collection p. 53 left.
Snark International/Edimedia p. 54 left.
British Library/Bridgeman Art Library p. 57 left.
Biblioteca Medicea Laurenziana, Florence Plut 61.10 c. 336v p. 57 right.
Dr Geoffrey King/SOAS p. 61 right.
The Publishers would also like to thank the following for permission to reproduce copyright material:
Heinemann Publishers Ltd for the extract from *Understanding History, Book I* by Child/Taylor/Shuter.
Every effort has been made to trace and acknowledge ownership of copyright. The Publishers will be glad to make suitable arrangements with any copyright holders whom it has not been possible to contact.

Many thanks to Marie Mellors and other library staff at the University of Wolverhampton, Clare Weaver, the staff at the British Library and Stuart Scott.

To our mothers, Ursula Michaels and Mildred Slater.

Illustrations by Joseph McEwan

British Library Cataloguing in Publication Data

Bartley, Paula
    Medieval Islam. – (Past Historic Series)
    I. Title II. Bourdillon, Hilary
    III. Series
    909.097671

    ISBN 0-340-52435-9

First published 1993

© 1993 Paula Bartley and Hilary Bourdillon

Typeset by Litho Link Ltd, Welshpool, Powys, Wales.
Printed in Hong Kong for the educational publishing division of Hodder and Stoughton Ltd, Mill Road, Dunton Green, Sevenoaks, Kent by Colorcraft Ltd.

CONTENTS

1 Introduction   4
2 The Growth of Islam   6
3 The Expansion of the Islamic Empire   12
4 Islamic Spain   14
5 Life in the Empire   18
6 Living in a Town   24
7 Life at Home   28
8 Eating Food   30
9 Non-Muslims in Islamic Lands   32
10 Keeping Healthy   34
11 Science and Technology   40
12 Art   44
13 Education   46
14 Leisure   48
15 Wars With the Christians   52
16 The Crusaders: Invaders or Heroes?   56
17 The Mongols and Ottomans   58
18 Why Islam Developed   60
19 Change and Continuity   62
   Glossary   64
   Index   65

Whenever Muslims speak or write Muhammad's name, they usually add, 'Peace be upon him' (sometimes written as 'pbuh'). It is a sign of respect. This book does not do so, but this is not intended to be disrespectful. A Muslim who reads aloud from this book may wish to add these words wherever the Prophet's name occurs.

INTRODUCTION

Islam began about 1,400 years ago in what is now called Saudi Arabia. This new religion spread far beyond this country. The map below shows the Islamic empire in the 8th century. Today it is one of the world's largest religions. Using this book you will be able to discover the reasons for the growth of Islam.

You will also find out about the Muslim religion and the importance of this to everyday life. Islam developed its own art, science and technology which you will also study.

A wide variety of primary and secondary sources have been used to write this book. There are many problems in writing a book about people living a long time ago in a different country.

- Some of the sources were written and drawn by Europeans whilst others were written and drawn by Muslims. The Muslim sources have been translated into English.
- Books and pictures are often held in libraries or record offices which are not easy to get into. Many Islamic sources are only available in Arab countries.
- It is difficult to uncover the lives of ordinary people because so few could read or write. Most written sources describe the activities of a very small number of people.
- Many primary sources have been lost or destroyed.

Primary sources were written or drawn by people living at the time. Secondary sources were written or drawn by people who lived long afterwards.

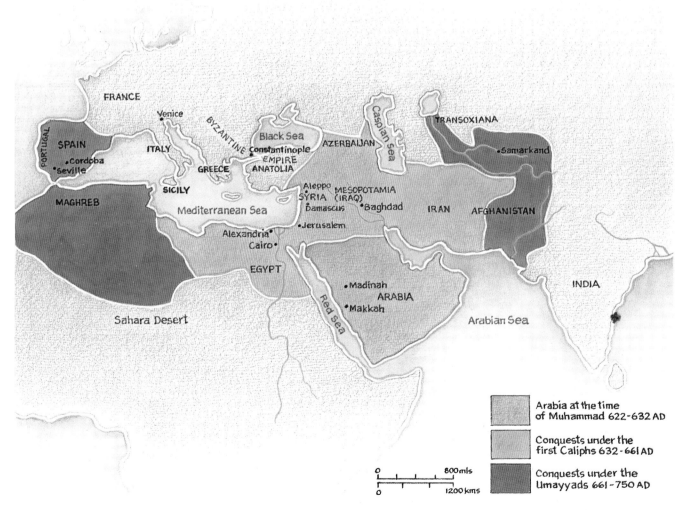

Arabia at the time of Muhammad 622-632 AD

Conquests under the first Caliphs 632-661 AD

Conquests under the Umayyads 661-750 AD

A   Map of the Islamic empire in the 8th century.

B Dome of the Rock, a place of worship, built in the 7th century, photographed recently.

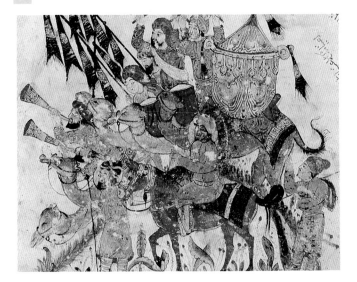

C *Chronicles of the Crusades* (1989) printed this caption below this picture:
Saracen forces in the field. Atop the camels ride kettledrummers, beating the drums which signalled the final assault on the city of Acre.

Early Islam (1969) printed this caption beneath this picture:
A party of joyous pilgrims sets out for the holy city: one of their number is a wealthy lady, riding discreetly in a tent-like litter.

1 Look at source B.
a) Is this modern photograph of any value to a historian researching medieval Islam? Give reasons.
b) This mosque is still used today. What does this tell you about the Muslim religion?
2 Look at source C and read the captions. Two books, both secondary sources, have given different captions to the same picture.
a) Give reasons why the authors might have written these captions.
b) What can these different captions tell us about the difficulty of finding out about medieval Islam?
c) How could we find out which of these captions is correct?
d) What other difficulties do historians face in writing about this period?
e) If finding sources is such a problem, should a book like this be written? Give reasons.

THE GROWTH OF ISLAM

500	600	700	800	900	1000	1100	1200	1300	1400	1500	1600

EARLY BEGINNINGS

Islam was founded by Muhammad who was born in the city of Makkah in about 571. He was an orphan brought up by his grandfather and his uncle.

At the age of 25 he married his employer, Khadijah, who was aged about 40. Khadijah and Muhammad had four daughters and two sons. Khadijah was a very successful business woman. Even though Muhammad could not read or write, Khadijah made Muhammad one of her managers. Muhammad ran her business extremely well, so they both lived very comfortably.

Muhammad was a religious man who often went into the mountains to pray. One day, whilst praying alone in a cave, Muhammad heard a voice. It was the voice of Gabriel, the Archangel, who gave Muhammad an important message from God. Gabriel told Muhammad that he was now God's messenger and he had to persuade people to obey God's commands.

This experience changed Muhammad's life and the lives of many others. For the next 23 years of his life Muhammad received many messages from God. All of the messages were printed firmly on his mind. These messages were written down and after Muhammad's death they were collected together. This was the *Qur'an*. The word *Qur'an* means to read or recite. Another important source for Muslims is called *Hadith*. This contains reports of what Muhammad said or did.

B A page from a 15th-century Qur'an.

Some people in Makkah listened carefully to Muhammad's ideas. They became Muslims. Others rejected his teachings because they still believed in many different gods.

When Khadijah died some of Muhammad's enemies tried to kill him. In fear of his life, Muhammad fled to Madinah in 622. Madinah was an oasis about 600 kilometres to the north of Makkah. This emigration from Makkah to Madinah is known as the *Hijra*, which means departure.

Muslims number their centuries from this date. They talk about the time before Hijra (BH) and the time after Hijra (AH).

A Mount Hira near Makkah. Muhammad was in a cave on Mount Hira when an angel appeared to him with a message from God.

C A Turkish painting from the 16th century showing the people of Madinah welcoming the arrival of Muhammad.

People in Madinah listened to Muhammad's teachings. Different tribes, such as the Awss and the Khazrajs, lived in Madinah but they were always arguing with each other. Muhammad helped to stop this fighting by building a community where everyone believed in the same religion and shared the same values. In return, these tribes helped Muhammad to fight his enemies in Makkah. Eventually in 630 they took control of this important city. The House of Prayer in Makkah called the Ka'abah became the most holy building in Islam.

D Anton Powell, *The Rise of Islam* (1979):
When he was about 25 he married a woman called Khadija, who was about 15 years older than himself. They had several children.

E John C Allen, *Muhammad and the Rise of Islam* (1973):
She made him a proposal of marriage which he accepted and they were married in A.D. 595, when Muhammad was 25. Although Khadija was fifteen years older than Muhammad, their marriage proved to be happy, and they had several children – two sons who died in infancy and four daughters.

1 The following statements describe events from Muhammad's life. Write them into your books in the correct order. (a) Muhammad receives his first message from God. (b) People in Madinah welcome Muhammad. (c) The birth of Muhammad. (d) Muhammad returns to Makkah. (e) The marriage of Muhammad and Khadijah.

2 Source C was painted by a Turkish artist in the 16th century. How useful is it to the historian as evidence of Muhammad's religious experience?

3 Read the text and sources D and E. Do you think Khadijah was really 40 when she married Muhammad? Give reasons for your answer.

4 The way people measure time is closely linked to their religion. Find out how Jews and Christians measure time.

MOSQUES

Muhammad's home at Madinah was the first mosque. It was a very simple building with a courtyard surrounded by walls of mud dried by the sun. To protect worshippers from the fierce sun, it was partly covered by a roof made of leaves and clay, held up by palm trunks.

Later mosques were very splendid buildings. When the Muslims conquered Syria, Iraq and Egypt they ruled over people who had already built beautiful places of worship. Sometimes they converted these buildings into mosques but they also built large and impressive new mosques.

People in different countries designed their own mosques using local materials. Mosques were built of mud in West Africa, from stone in Tunisia. The modern mosque in Regent's Park, London is made of brick and cement. Although mosques were built from different materials they can be easily recognised.

A The mosque in Regent's Park, London.

B Ibn Battuta, a traveller (1304-69), described the Dome of the Rock mosque in Jerusalem.

The Dome of the Rock is a building of extraordinary beauty and elegance. It is reached by a flight of steps. It has four doors. The space round it is also paved with marble, excellently done. Both outside and inside the decoration is magnificent. The greater part is covered with gold so that the eyes are dazzled by its brilliance. This gold glows brightly and flashes like lightning in the sun. In the centre of the Dome is the blessed rock from which the Prophet ascended to heaven.

C Preaching in a mosque. This was painted in 1237.

D An 18th-century painting of Makkah. The mosque and the Ka'abah (see page 10) are in the centre.

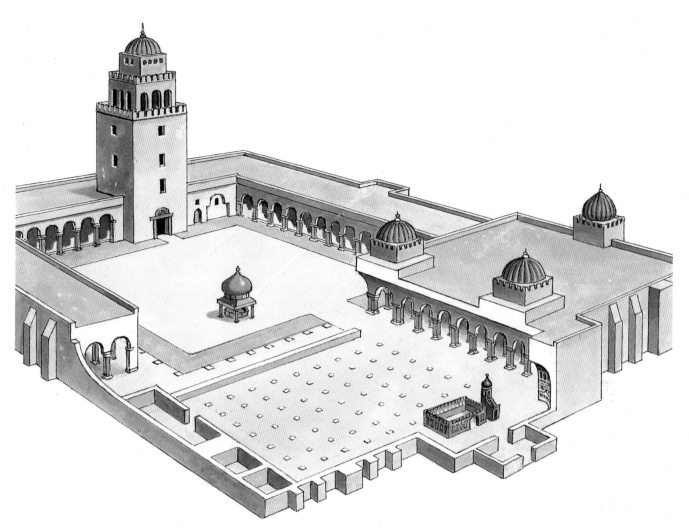

E A plan of a mosque.

Mosques usually have a dome and a tall tower called the minaret. Traditionally, a muezzin calls the people to prayer from the top of the tower. Nowadays a loudspeaker is often used instead. A minbar, a raised platform, is used on Fridays by the imam to preach.

There is an open courtyard with a fountain in the middle so people can wash before they pray. After they are clean, Muslims go into the covered prayer hall where they worship on richly decorated carpets. There are no seats. As Muslims always pray facing Makkah, a small archway called a mihrab points towards the holy city. Around the wall of the mosque there are usually quotations from the Qur'an, written in beautiful handwriting.

All over the world – in Egypt, in Britain, in Saudi Arabia and America – Muslims worship in their own particular mosque. Friday is the holiest day for Muslims. Every Friday most men and boys visit the mosque to pray. Women are allowed to attend the services but they can also stay and pray at home. Men and women pray separately in the mosque.

Facts are statements which we can prove are true. You can, for instance, count the doors in a mosque. Opinions are someone's point of view. They are not always true.

1 Look at source A. What evidence is there to suggest that it is a mosque?

2 Copy source E and mark in all the parts of a mosque. Use the text to help you.

3 a) Read source B. Write down all the facts in this source.
b) Write down the words that contain the opinion of the author.

4 a) Look at the numbered people and objects in source C. Who is 1?
b) What is 2 and 3?
c) What do you think 4 is doing?

5 Why do mosques differ so much in various countries?

BELIEFS AND PRACTICES

Jews, Christians and Muslims all believe in one God. Muslims call God, *Allah*. Allah sent messages through the teachings of the prophets. Abraham, Moses and John the Baptist were all prophets. So, too, was Jesus, although Muslims do not believe he was the son of God.

For Muslims, Muhammad is the last of a long line of prophets. He is God's final messenger on earth. The message taught that every Muslim should keep five rules. These are called the five pillars of Islam.

1	2	3	4	5
To believe in one God whose messenger is Muhammad	To pray five times a day	To give to the poor	To fast during Ramadan	To make a pilgrimage, called the Hajj, to Makkah

A The five pillars of Islam.

B The Ka'abah at Makkah. Ka'abah means cube. This was an old religious shrine which Muslims believe was built by Abraham nearly 4,000 years ago. It is situated in the mosque at Makkah.

Ramadan is the ninth month of the Muslim year. It is the month in which Muhammad received a message from God. Ramadan lasts for 30 days. During this time Muslims are not allowed to eat or drink from just before dawn to just after dusk. People such as pregnant women, children and soldiers who are marching do not have to fast like this.

All Muslims, rich and poor, are supposed to visit Makkah, the holiest of Islamic cities, when they have enough money. Someone who has made the pilgrimage to Makkah is called a hajji (male) or hajja (female). From a certain point in their journey, each pilgrim dresses alike in a white cloth. Rich people and poor people all look the same. This is to make sure that everyone is seen as equal before the eyes of God.

Wherever a Muslim lives, he or she says prayers in Arabic. They also pray in certain positions; they are the same for all Muslims everywhere.

Muslims are encouraged to give to charity. Every Muslim must pay a tax, called a zakat, which is often one-fortieth of their earnings and goes to the poor.

C A pilgrimage to Makkah. Some pilgrims go to Makkah every year. On the last few days of the pilgrimage there is a festival parade. This picture, drawn in 1287 in Baghdad, shows musicians preparing for the festival parade in Makkah.

D Pilgrims arriving in Makkah today.

Quotations from the Qur'an

E A good deed and an evil deed are not alike: repay evil with something that is finer, and see how someone who is separated from you by hatred will become a bosom friend.
Set Forth in Detail 41: 33-36

F Those who spend their wealth night and day, both privately and publicly, will receive their earnings from their Lord. No fear will lie upon them nor need they ever feel saddened.
The Cow 2: 274

G God's curse will rest on him if he is a liar.
The Light 24:7

H You who will believe, liquor and gambling, idols and raffles, are only a filthy work of Satan; avoid them so that you may prosper.
The Table 5: 90-91

I God has permitted trading and forbidden taking interest.
The Cow 2: 275

J God alone holds control over Heaven and Earth.
The Cow 2: 107

K God is the One Who created Heaven and Earth as well as whatever lies between them, in six days.
Worship 32: 4-9

L Muhammad is not the father of any of your men, but he is God's messenger.
The Confederates 33: 40

M Do not commit adultery. It is a shameful and evil way to act.
The Night Journey 17: 22-39

N Give full measure whenever you measure anything, and weigh with proper scales; that is better and the finest way of acting.
The Night Journey 17: 22:39

O You who believe, whenever you intend to pray, wash your faces and your hands up to the elbows, and wipe your head and wash your feet up to the ankles.
The Table 5: 6

P The month of Ramadan is when the Qur'an was sent down as guidance for mankind, and with explanation for guidance, and as a Standard. Let any of you who is at home during the month, fast in it.
The Cow 2: 183-187

Q Pilgrimage to the House (the Ka'abah) is a duty imposed on mankind by God for anyone who can afford a way to do so.
The House of Imran 3: 97

---

1 Read all of the quotations from the Qur'an.
   a) Draw a chart using the headings below:
   one God   prayer   alms   fasting   hajj
   Put each of the sayings under the five pillars of Islam.
   b) Which sayings do not fit under the five pillars?
   c) What can you learn about the life of Muslims from these other sayings?
   d) Which of the five pillars is shown in sources C and D?

2 Look at source C and source D. What has changed and what has remained the same about pilgrimages to Makkah?

500	600	700	800	900	1000	1100	1200	1300	1400	1500	1600

As long as Muhammad lived he was a prophet, a judge, commander of the army and the head of state. When he died in 632 there was no one to take over his leadership. Muhammad left no male children but he had one daughter called Fatimah.

Abu-Bakr, who was aged about 60, was Muhammad's father-in-law. After a lot of disagreement, Abu-Bakr became the first caliph, which meant that he ruled over the Islamic empire. Caliphs were leaders of the community, like Muhammad, but they were not God's messengers.

Led by the caliphs, Islam became a great empire. Different caliphs began their own line of rulers called dynasties. The main dynasties and development of Islam are shown below. You will read more about all of these developments in this book.

610-632 – ISLAM UNDER MUHAMMAD

Islam is established by Muhammad in Makkah and Madinah.

632-661 – THE RIGHTLY GUIDED CALIPHS

The first four caliphs are known as the Rightly Guided Caliphs. Three of them were murdered.

661-750 – THE CALIPHATE OF THE UMAYYADS

The Umayyads made Islam even bigger. Islamic culture was founded in all the places they conquered. Under the caliph, Mu'awiya, Damascus in Syria became the capital of the Islamic empire in 661.

From about 690, Arabic became the official language of government. At the same time new religious coins were minted which had words on them praising God and Islam. The first great mosque, the Dome of the Rock in Jerusalem, was built in the 690s. Mosques were built in many towns, for example, Damascus, Aleppo and Madinah.

750-1055 – THE CALIPHATE OF THE ABBASIDS

After a civil war the Abbasid family came to power. Abu'l Abbas became the first Abbasid caliph. Arabic language became the official language in all the countries of the Islamic empire. The Abbasids made Iraq, instead of Syria, the centre of the empire. Baghdad was founded as the

new capital in 763 by al-Mansur. It remained a powerful city until 1258 when it was destroyed by the Mongols.

Baghdad led the known world in new ideas. The science of astronomy was brought to Baghdad in about 771 from India. Stories such as the Arabian Nights began to be told in about 786.

1055-1258 – THE CALIPHATE OF THE SELDJUKS

A wave of invasions by Turkish wandering tribes changed the Islamic empire. In 1091 the Seldjuks made Baghdad their capital city. Pope Urban began the first Crusade in 1096. By 1118 the Seldjuk empire had broken up into small states. Between 1171-93, Saladin ruled.

1258-1517 – THE MAMLUKS

Mongol tribes from Central Asia invaded the Islamic world. Baghdad was destroyed in 1258 by Hulegu. The centre of Islamic life moved out of Iraq to Cairo in Egypt and Damascus in Syria.

Chronology means putting events in date order. The earliest date should come first.

1 Look at source A. What are 1, 2, 3, 4, 5, 6, and 7? The following sentences will help you.
a) This man is the caliph. Just behind him is a man holding a mace which is a symbol of authority.
b) Cooking kebabs.
c) Court officials included official tasters. This man is tasting sherbet to see if it has been poisoned before the caliph drinks it.
d) A guard.
e) These people are having fun. Can you see the baby? Can you see the camel? Some of the people are playing polo. There is a polo stick in the middle of the picture.
f) Cleaners.
g) Soldiers hunting.

2 Put these sentences into the correct chronological order:
(i) Cairo becomes the capital city;
(ii) Damascus becomes the capital city;
(iii) Arabic becomes the official language;
(iv) Baghdad is founded;
(v) First Crusade begins.

A Islam was ruled by a caliph who was believed to be God's representative on earth. This picture shows scenes of the caliph's court around 1250. You can see that every person has a halo. This does not mean they are saints. Muslim artists liked the look of halos which Christian artists painted around holy people. They copied the style and painted halos around everyone.

4 ISLAMIC SPAIN

500	600	700	800	900	1000	1100	1200	1300	1400	1500	1600

If you were to visit a town like Seville in southern Spain today and looked at the cathedrals there, you would be in for a surprise. In Seville Cathedral you can see the impressive tomb of Christopher Columbus who sailed across the Atlantic in 1492 and began the European exploration of the Americas.

Behind the main altar is a huge screen, made with the gold the Spaniards brought from South America. All over the cathedral are statues to the Virgin Mary and other Christian saints. But if you climbed up the Cathedral tower you would discover that this was not built to be part of a great church.

The tower is, in fact, a minaret, built by the Muslims in the 12th century. From the top of the minaret, you can see the Alcazar, the palace built in the 13th century for the Muslim rulers of Spain. It was later made into a palace for the kings of Spain. At the top of the tower in Seville Cathedral you are in the middle of an Arabic town.

B Seville Cathedral. The cathedral 'tower' as it is today.

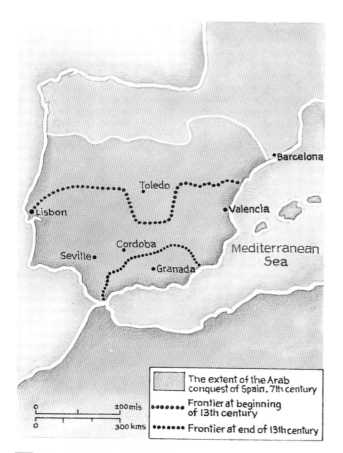

A The Muslims in Spain.

In 711, the Muslims invaded Spain, which they called al-Andalus. The conquerors were the Umayyad caliphs who ruled from Damascus. In 750, the Muslims, led by the Abbasids in Syria, massacred the Umayyads. They did not think the Umayyads were suitable to be Muhammad's successors. The Abbasids took over.

One Umayyad prince escaped and went to Spain. His relatives ruled Spain after him. Their capital was Cordoba.

Muslims ruled in parts of Spain until the end of the 15th century. Spain has a long Muslim history. It is not always easy to find this history because Christians took over the mosques and other buildings to use as churches and palaces.

C A publicity leaflet advertising a new book called *Understanding History* (1991), describes the Muslim invasion of Spain:

The Arabs intended to conquer the world and convert it to Islam. Western Europe was one of the main targets. In 711, they invaded Spain from North Africa and conquered most of it. In 720, they crossed the Pyrenees Mountains and pushed into France. By 732 they had got as far as Tours, some 200 miles from the English Channel. This was as far as they got. At the Battle of Poitiers (732) they were defeated and driven out of France. They were not driven out of Spain, however. Arab rule of southern Spain was to last another 750 years.

D W Montgomery Watt, *The Influence of Islam on Medieval Europe* (1972):

There is a temptation for the historian of Europe after he has given an account of the invasions by Germans and Slavs, Magyars and Norsemen, to think of the Arab conquests of Spain as the same 'barbarian' invasion. The Arabs were representatives of an empire which in the next century or two became the bearer of the highest culture and civilisation in the whole vast region from the Atlantic to Afghanistan.

E The Alcazar, Seville. This was built by Arab craftspeople employed by Christians who had taken over Seville.

Muslim culture, architecture, religion, agriculture, science and literature were brought to Spain and eventually to the rest of Europe. The Arabs brought irrigation to Spain. Crops which needed a lot of water could now be grown. They included sugar-cane, rice, oranges, artichokes, apricots and cotton.

The rich in Muslim Spain had a very luxurious life. Fine textiles, woollens and silk were made to use at home and to sell abroad.

Spanish leather work was thought to be the best at this time. Boots, bags and even wall coverings were highly decorated by craftspeople. Inlaid silver and other metal work was also of a remarkable standard.

Spain was the first country in Europe to use paper. This knowledge was passed on to Christian Europe. Even the Spanish guitar was brought to Spain by Islamic musicians.

In the late 800s, the glassmakers in Cordoba discovered how to make crystal . Wonderful necklaces, bracelets and earrings all showed the wealth of Spain and the skill of its goldsmiths and jewellers.

F Alvaro, a 9th-century Spanish Christian bishop wrote:

Many of my priests read the poetry and tales of the Arabs, study the writings of Muhammad, not to argue against them but to learn how to speak correctly in Arabic. Where can you find anyone who reads Latin, who studies the Bible? Young Christians know only the language and literature of the Arabs, read and study Arabic books. There is hardly one who can write a good Latin letter to a friend but many can write in Arabic.

When they write history, historians are influenced by the ideas of the time in which they live. Many European historians have ignored the history of non-Christian Europeans. In the middle ages many Christian historians were monks and they wrote history from the Church's point of view.

1 a) What point does the writer of source D make about how Europeans see the history of Spain?
b) What impression of the Muslim invasion of Spain does source C give?

2 What does source E tell us about the influence of Islam on Christian Spain?

3 Read source F.
a) What is Alvaro concerned about?
b) Why do you think that he is so worried?
c) What might a Muslim say in reply?

CORDOBA

The Great Mosque at Cordoba.

Forty-four years after the conquest of Spain, Abd al-Rahman, an Umayyad, built the city of Cordoba. This capital city was thought to be the best city in Europe and the third best in the world.

Unlike the dirty, smelly cities of Europe, Cordoba was an hygienic and healthy place to live. About 300 public baths kept the people of the city clean. Miles of paved streets were lit up at night from the lights of the houses nearby. Richer houses even had their own piped water.

Grand palaces were built from Italian marble. The Royal Palace had about 400 rooms and apartments. It took about 10,000 workers 25 years to build it.

Rooms in this palace had marble walls decorated with gold. The main door arch was made of ebony, a rich black wood, and ivory set with jewels.

Not surprisingly, Cordoba had many, many mosques. It is said that there were about 700 mosques dotted around the city to make sure that every Muslim could worship easily.

One mosque was as big as 20 hockey pitches. Inside this impressive building was a university which attracted students from all over Europe and the Islamic world. Christians, Jews and Muslims all studied here.

B Al Rasi, a Spanish historian, said in 935:
Cordoba is the mother of cities, the seat of royalty, its river is the largest in al-Andalus; its bridge is the wonder of the world in its architecture and design; its mosque is second to none in al-Andalus.

C al-Hijari was a Spanish historian who died in 1188. He wrote:
Cordoba after the conquest of Spain, became the headquarters of the army, mother of all towns, home of the good and pious , and the home of clever and educated people. Seekers of science and poetry all came to Cordoba for it was a place of the noble and the learned. In it writers competed with warriors, and the nobility mixed with the army.

Cordoba had many beautiful books. The people of Cordoba are better than any others [because] people are interested in asking questions and learning about science and literature.

After the death of al-Mansur, the great ruler of Cordoba in 1002, Muslim Spain broke up into many small kingdoms. The Christians in the north saw this as their chance to invade. One of the most famous Christian leaders was Rodrigo Diaz de Vivar, better known as *El Cid*.

In 1094, he conquered Valencia. It took several hundred years before the Christians pushed the Muslims out of Spain. In 1492, the last Muslim kingdom of Granada was captured by Queen Isabella of Spain. At first the Christians treated the Muslims generously, but, by 1502, Muslims had to choose either to become a Christian or to leave the country.

1 a) Read sources B and C.
   What reasons are given why Cordoba is a wonderful place to live?
   b) Give three other reasons why someone might want to live in Cordoba.
   c) Put all the reasons in order of importance.
   d) Write a few paragraphs on why people wanted to live in Cordoba, using your answers to (a), (b) and (c) to help you.
2 How do you think Muslim influence might have spread as a result of the Spanish conquest? Think about education, architecture, science and literature to help you decide.
3 a) Look at source D.
   Which is the Christian army and which is the Muslim? Give reasons.
   b) Make up a caption for the picture from the Muslim point of view and another caption from the Christian point of view.

D This picture dates from the 15th century. It is Spanish. It shows Christians fighting against the Muslims. The Muslims are planning to attack a city. They surround a Christian army (the ones carrying the crosses and the picture of the Virgin Mary) who fight and escape.

5

LIFE IN THE EMPIRE

GROWING FOOD

Olive trees provided food, cooking oil and fuel. Wheat and other cereal crops were grown to make bread and provide food for animals. Palm trees were grown for the dates. These were the three basic crops. Each grew in a different area of the Muslim world according to what the climate was like.

Some parts of the empire grew lots of food. In parts of Persia and Iraq it was possible to grow food all the year round. Here, people lived a settled life working on the land.

In other parts of the empire, in the dry desert areas, there was only enough rain to grow grass for camels. Camels can travel long distances in the heat without having to drink and people moved from one area to another all the time to find fresh grazing. They had only one meal a day. Some historians argue that this pushed the Arabs to move into new areas in search of food.

Much farming was only possible because farmers could water their land. The Arabs developed ways of irrigating the land.

December
Winter cropping
● last sowing of barley
● sowing of wheat, linseed and lentils

Summer cropping
● late picking of cotton
● uprooting cotton plants
● burning the old roots for compost
● ploughing and harrowing the fields for fallowing

Trees
● manuring grapes, vines and other trees
● planting chestnut during second half of month
● collecting the produce of olive and quince trees

Historians have to try to work out how reliable historical sources are. In order to do this they have to ask who produced the source and why they produced it. For example, they have to ask whether a handbook on how to farm is as reliable as say a diary written by a farmer, about farming methods. Does the advice given in a modern book on gardening accurately describe gardens in the 1990s?

A A book on farming, written by Ibn-al-Nabatiyya who lived in Iraq in the 9th century, gives this advice to farmers:

May
Winter cropping
● harvesting barley
● harvesting wheat and linseed in the later part of the month
● harvesting chick-peas and lentils
● harvesting flax

Summer cropping
● preparation of land for planting rice and millet
● planting rice and millet and the early sowing of sesame
● late planting cotton
● weeding cotton
● gathering melons, cucumber, peas, beans, broad-beans and okra

Trees
● bedding nursery plants
● grafting grape-vines
● hoeing around trees
● manuring orchards

Okra: this is sometimes called Lady's Fingers. It is eaten in stews or on its own as a vegetable.

Sesame: the seeds are used in cooking. Oil is squeezed from the seeds.

Quince: a fruit which is made into jams, jellies and pies.

B Some of the foods grown in Iraq in the 9th century.

When Arab officials went to rule other parts of the empire, they took with them their favourite food. Oranges and lemons were taken to Spain. Almonds were grown wherever possible. Rice and sugar cane from India were planted. Even the saffron, which gave food a rich golden glow, was soon used from the east to the west of the Mediterranean.

C Farmers at work. This picture is taken from a manuscript probably drawn in northern Iraq in 1199.

1 a) What does source A tell you about farming in Iraq?
b) Does it tell you anything about people's diets? Explain your answer.
c) Make a list of all the different ways mentioned here of fertilising the land.
d) Was the land used all the year round, or not? Explain your answer.

2 How reliable do you think source A is? In what ways is the fact that it is a book written to give advice to farmers significant to the historian? Give reasons for your answer.

3 a) Look at source C. Make a list of the activities shown at 1, 2, 3 and 4 in the picture.
b) Make a list of all the tools being used.
c) What evidence is there in the picture that northern Iraq was a rich farming region?

SUQS (MARKETS)

Each town had at least one ▢suq▢. Large towns had many of them scattered throughout the town. Suqs sold all sorts of goods. Streets specialised in different goods. Some streets only sold candles, whereas other streets sold books. All of the trades were kept separate.

weights and measures. When they did not, punishment was severe. One shop owner in Egypt who had cheated on his customers had a notice put on him and was forced to ride through the streets on a camel. He rang a bell to let everyone know about his crime.

A A suq, drawn in the 13th century.

The cleanest and most important trades were near the mosque. Here you could find the candle, ▢incense▢ and perfume merchants. The pleasant smells of these goods floated around this most sacred of buildings. Grouped around them were the booksellers, the cloth-sellers, the tailors and carpet merchants. Next came the food merchants, who sold wheat, beans, chick peas, onions, garlic and fruit. Then came the blacksmiths and the potters. Farthest away from the mosque were the smelliest trades of all, such as leather work.

This practice of keeping each craft separate was introduced by the Umayyad caliphs. It soon spread to other places as far afield as India, Persia, Iraq and Egypt. This system made it easier for the caliphs to keep control of the different trades.

No article was ever marked with a price. If people wanted to buy perfume, food or even a piece of cloth they bargained with the shop keeper. You could not rush into a shop to buy some bread. People talked for a long time before they reached an agreement. It was impossible to shop in the suqs quickly.

Each trade belonged to an *asnaf* or guild. This made sure that the shops did not over-charge their customers. Shop keepers also had to ensure that the goods they sold were of a decent quality.

An inspector made sure that shop owners did not cheat. Each trade was expected to use correct

B Yakubi, a visitor to Baghdad in about 900 said:
Here every merchant, and each merchandise, had an appointed street: and there were rows of shops, and of booths, and of courts, in each of those streets; but men of one business were not mixed up with those of another . . . Goods of a kind were only sold with their kind, and men of one trade were not to be found except with their fellows of the same craft. Thus each market was kept single.

C Ibn Batuta (1304-1369), another traveller, wrote:
Near the mosque we will find the suq of the booksellers, the suq of the bookbinders, and, as its neighbour, the suq of the leather merchants and the makers of slippers.

Approaching the gates of the town one will find the makers of saddles and those of pack-saddles whose customers are country people. Then the food sellers together with the basket makers. At the edge of the town because they require space and because they are thought undesirable: the dyers, the ▢tanners▢, and almost outside the city limits, the potters.

D Ibn Agil writing in 1119 said:
In the market places . . . the perfumers did not mix with the merchants of greasy and other offensive smells, nor did the merchants of new articles mix with those of used articles.

E A suq in present-day Morocco.

A visit to a market today will tell you a lot about people's lifestyle. For example, the building of large supermarkets and car parks on the outskirts of towns tells us that people drive to the supermarkets to do their shopping, loading up their cars so they don't have to shop more than once a week. The appearance of organic food is a sign that people are becoming concerned about the quality of their food. Markets in the past are also valuable sources of information about the lifestyle of people living at that time.

1 a) What reasons does the text give for why the trades were kept separate?
b) What reasons do the sources give for why the trades were kept separate?
c) Why do you think leather sellers and dyers were near the city walls?
d) Why do you think bookbinders were near the mosque?
e) Read source C. Do you think it is sensible for trades to be kept separate? Give reasons.

2 Look at source A. Which shop is: (a) the jeweller's; (b) the butcher's; (c) the chemist? Explain how you decided.
3 Look at source E.
a) Why might this modern picture be useful to a historian studying town life in Islam in the middle ages?
b) What are the limitations in using this picture as evidence for this?
4 What does the information given in this chapter tell you about Muslim society?

MERCHANTS AND TRADERS

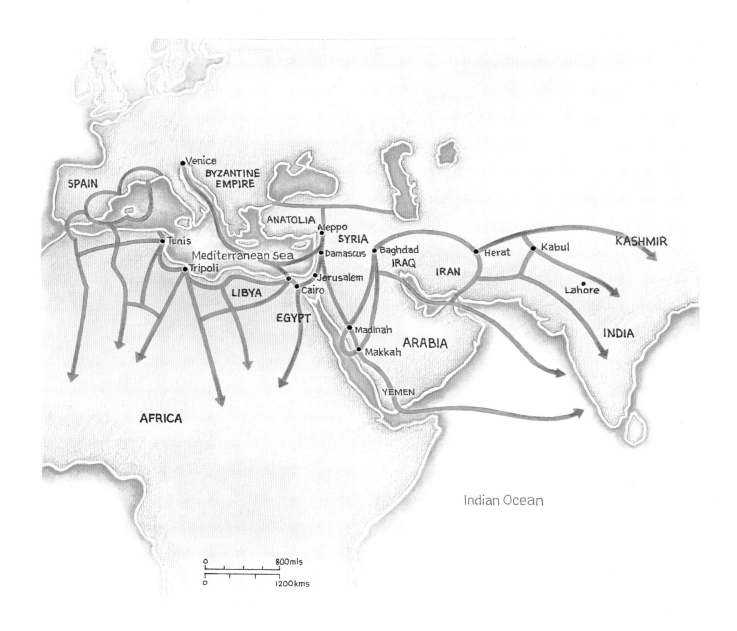

A Arab trade routes. From the information given on this map, how do you think the Arab merchants travelled from one country to another?

Before the Muslims moved into the Mediterranean, trade was dangerous. People attacked strangers, stole their goods and sometimes murdered them. The Muslims brought peace to this area and the fighting stopped. Trade became easier. It was also helped by the spread of the Arabic language. A century or so after the conquests, Christians, Jews and Zorastrians in the Muslim empire spoke and wrote Arabic.

Goods could be bought and sold easily because a system of banking developed. Money was loaned to people to buy goods. The idea of the cheque comes from the Arabic bankers. It was possible for a cheque to be written in one part of the empire and cashed in a distant city. The use of gold and silver currency also made trade easy. In the east the silver Persian coin, the Dirham, was used. In the west the currency was the gold Dinarius.

The best business of all to be in was trekking with the camel caravans. Great caravans travelled overland through central Asia to Baghdad, then they went to North Africa and the Mediterranean ports of Spain.

B Ibn Khaldun, writer and historian (1332-1406).
It will bring the merchant more profit if he brings goods from a country that is far away and where there is danger on the road. Therefore the merchant who dares to enter into the Sudan country will be the wealthiest of all people. The distance and difficulty of the roads they travel are great. They have to cross a desert which it is almost impossible to cross because of the fear of danger and great thirst. Therefore the goods of the Sudan country are found only in small quantities, and they are particularly expensive.

C The Caravanserais of Mahyar in Iran. Caravanserais were built to provide stops for the caravans. Travellers could stay at them free for three days. Meals were also free. The same food was served to all – Muslims, Christians, rich or poor, free person or slave. Larger caravanserais treated the sick.

Who were the Merchants?

What type of person was the merchant? What made a successful merchant?

D Ibn Khaldun (1332-1406) wrote:
It is unavoidable that there should be cheating and tampering with merchandise which may ruin them. All this causes the merchant a great deal of trouble. If he is not afraid of quarrels, knows how to settle an account, and is always willing to enter into a dispute and go to court, he stands a better chance of being treated fairly because he is not afraid.

Otherwise he must have the protection of being an important person. This will bring him respect in the eyes of the traders and will cause the   magistrate   to support him against the people who owe him money.

E A merchant prepares to take off on a great overland journey (1237). Camels could travel very long distances without the need for a drink. In desert sand storms, the camel can close its nostrils and eyelashes to protect it from the sand.

___

1 a) Make a list of what caused trade to grow in the Muslim empire.
   b) Put these reasons into the order which you think is the most important. Explain why you have put them into that order.
2 Read source B. Why does the merchant make most money by trading with a country which is far away?
3 a) What does source E tell you about merchants in the Muslim empire?
   b) What does source D tell you about them?

   c) Using the evidence from all the text and the sources, what qualities were needed to be a successful Arab merchant at this time?
4 A person's place in Muslim society depended on how wealthy they were.
   a) What might poorer people have thought about this?
   b) What did rich people think about this?
   c) What effect did this have on Muslim society?

6

LIVING IN A TOWN

Muslims preferred to live in towns rather than in the country. Town life allowed Muslims to lead a life of which Muhammad would have approved.

Many towns were surrounded by high walls. In the centre of each town was a mosque. Near to the mosque were the palaces and grand houses of royalty and government officials. This area was surrounded by the suq. Public baths were usually situated near the suq.

All around this was the residential district in which different religious groups lived separately. There would be a Jewish quarter, a Christian quarter and a Muslim quarter. Around all of these were the cemeteries.

To visit an Islamic town was to enter a world that appeared chaotic . There were no well-designed or attractive streets in which people could stroll on a sunny afternoon. People lived in narrow, winding, gloomy streets. These dark streets remained cool in the heat of the very hot day.

Each house was surrounded by high walls. In some places the roof tops touched each other. This made it difficult for anyone to see where they were going. Very little air circulated which made it quite unpleasant to breathe.

Only pack animals and people on foot used these streets. Carts or carriages would not have enough room. If you did not know your way around these streets it was very easy to get completely lost.

Although these towns looked dirty, this was not really the case. Muslims took hygiene very seriously. Some towns had reservoirs, some had aqueducts . Towns such as Antioch, which you can see marked on page 4, had plenty of running water. It was carried in small pipes to the richer houses to use for drinking and for the fountains.

In Egypt, water was carried by camel or people. A large number of camels were used, sometimes as many as 8,000. Each camel had a leather bag on its side containing the amount of water usually stored in a small barrel. In this way large cities such as Cairo had a fresh water supply.

A Ibn Khaldun (1332-1406) wrote:

The purpose of building towns is to have places for dwelling and shelter. Therefore, it is necessary to see to it that harmful things are kept away from the towns by protecting them. For the protection of towns, all the houses should be situated inside a surrounding wall. The town should be situated in a place which is difficult to reach, either upon a rugged hill or surrounded by the sea or by a river, so that it can be reached only by crossing some sort of bridge.

One should see that the air is wholesome, in order to be safe from illness. When the air is bad . . . all living beings who are there will speedily be affected by illness.

The place should be on a river, or near springs with plenty of fresh water.

One of the tasks of the historian is to find out why something happened. There are often different reasons for an event so they try to work out which is the most important.

1 Look at source B. Write down what you can see at the numbered places. The following words will help you: city walls, city gates, citadel, houses, mosque, moat.

2 a) Using both the text and the sources, write down as many reasons as you can why towns were built.
   b) List them in order of importance, explaining your choice.

3 Read the text and source A.
   a) How do they agree?

   b) How do they differ?
   c) Do you think the primary or the secondary text more accurate? Give reasons.
   d) If readers were only presented with the primary sources in this chapter how would that give a different idea of town life?

4 Find a book which contains information about town life in Europe at this time. How similar is it to town life in the Islamic empire?

The city of Aleppo in the 16th century.

BAGHDAD

A   Baghdad painted in 1468.

Baghdad was built by the Abbasid caliphs who ruled over the eastern part of the Islamic world from 750 until 1055. It was the capital of the empire. Over a million people lived there at a time when London had a population of just about 10,000. Baghdad was almost the largest city in the world until it was destroyed in 1258.

This impressive city lay between the two great rivers of the Tigris and Euphrates. Baghdad was built with great care. Every city in the whole of the caliph's empire had to send its finest craftspeople to help build Baghdad. About 100,000 people took four years to build it.

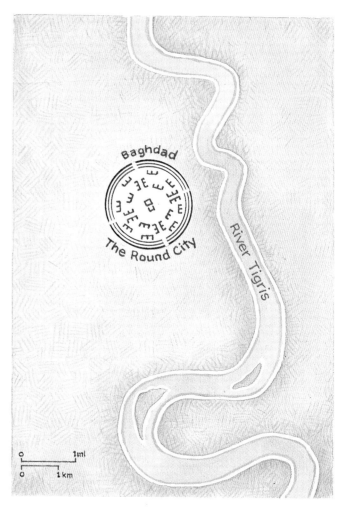

B   The round city of Baghdad.

Baghdad was built in a circle. Not surprisingly, it was called the round city. The city was surrounded by double brick walls about 90 feet (30 m) high with a deep moat filled with water from the Karkhaya canal.

In the middle of Baghdad stood the caliph's palace where the caliph, his wives, slaves, and body-guards lived. This palace was extremely large. Even the green dome of the palace was built so high that it could be seen miles away. It was known as the Palace of the Golden Gate. Nearby were smaller palaces where the caliph's children and servants lived. Next to the palace stood the mosque.

Historians rely on primary sources for their information. They do not believe everything a primary source says. Questions such as who made it, when was it made and why was it made are asked of each source. This is because historians want to understand the attitudes of the person who made the primary source.

C al-Katib al-Baghdadi (1002-71) wrote about it:
Inside the palace grew a tree, in the midst of a great circular tank filled with clear water. The tree has eighteen branches, every branch having numerous twigs, in which sit all sorts of gold and silver birds, both large and small.

Most of the branches of this tree are of silver, but some are of gold, and they spread into the air carrying leaves of different colours. The leaves of the tree move as the wind blows, while the birds pipe and sing.

D Ibn Batuta (1304-1369) described the city in *Travels in Asia and Africa*:
There is one street which closely follows the Tigris. On one of its sides, it has palaces overlooking the river, spread all the way from the Bridge to the beginning of the Zahir Garden. On the other side of the street are the mosques of the owners of these palaces, and the dwellings of their soldiers.

Close to this street, at the bridge, is Suq Yahya, which unites the palaces close to the river bank. The horses of these palaces eat daily fodder amounting to 1,000 nosebags. Then at the end of this suq there are the dwellings of pious men and their superiors.

Then there is the meeting place of learned men and poets and the wonderful water fountains on the road to the Mosque with their many caretakers.

On the west bank there are palaces, all with water-wheels, gardens and balconies facing across the Tigris. A vessel , in good trim, awaits the lord of the Palace, with beautiful finery and marvellous woodwork. And the ducks playfully swim together in the riverside palace.

Many a time would the singing voices of this quarter mix with the sounds of its waterwheels, the quacking of its ducks, the noisy voices of its soldiers and servants, while the Tigris gently streamed along between the two rows of its riverside palaces. And many a time did I sail along in a vessel, hearing these melodies sound all the way.

The people were always celebrating some event such as the circumcision of an infant boy, or the marrying of a woman. And on Saturdays there were readings from the Qur'an, fencing and wrestling shows, and boat racing.

One place called the Karkh has a number of wondrous dwellings of beautiful architecture. In it the wonderful palaces are located. There used to be a library containing 12,000 volumes.

E A drawing of the statue of a rider on top of the Green Dome.

1   Look at source B and read the text. Give as many reasons as you can why Baghdad was built near the Tigris and the Euphrates.

2   a) Using all the primary sources in this chapter, list all the evidence which shows that Baghdad was a splendid place to live.
b) From your knowledge of town life, do you think this evidence is accurate? Give reasons.

c) How has this evidence been influenced by the people who wrote or painted it? Explain your answer.

3   Using all the sources in this chapter, write a travel guide to Baghdad. Include the structure of the town, the buildings, the sights and sounds. You may illustrate it if you wish.

7 LIFE AT HOME

Poor people lived in huts around open courtyards or else in apartment houses. These houses often had workshops on the ground floor which led to the upstairs living rooms.

Richer people lived more grandly. Although the streets outside were noisy and dirty, inside the houses it was calm and clean. Home was a place of peace, away from the hustle and bustle of the town. The family was protected from all the noise and pollution outside.

Many houses were built around courtyards which had gardens and fountains gently sprinkling water. The garden was a cool and sweet smelling place. People sat on a carpet in their gardens to talk

A A house, painted in 1237.

B A 14th-century peaceful garden.

helped themselves from these dishes. Rich people had trays made of silver and wood inlaid with mother of pearl. Some ate with spoons and knives. Poorer people ate with their fingers using pieces of flat bread, like pitta bread, to help eat the mushy bits of food.

Richer families had servants to prepare and cook the food and to do the housework. This was the only work women could get in towns. Many of the women were slaves. Slavery was accepted in many countries at this time. They had rights in Muslim law. Slaves had to be treated kindly, be given medicines when they were ill and looked after when they became too old to work.

It was thought to be an act of great goodness to free a slave. Slave owners and slaves often developed a close friendship. Sometimes, slaves who had been given their freedom went into business with a former master, or even married a member of the family.

Only non-Muslims could be slaves. According to the law, a person could only be a slave if they were captured or if their parents were slaves. There was, however, a trade in slaves who were brought from East Africa. Most of them were women, although there was also a demand for male slaves to work on the land or to be soldiers.

C Edward William Lane, a 19th-century author, wrote this about Arabian society in the Middle Ages:

It is important to wash at least the right hand before eating with the fingers anything but dry food; and the mouth also is often rinsed.

The master of the house begins first: if he did not so, some persons would suspect that the food was poisoned. The thumb and two fingers of the right hand serve instead of knives and forks. Sometimes a host hands a delicate morsel with his fingers to one of his guests.

with their friends or to play games. Carpets were even designed to look like gardens. Muslims believed that Paradise would be a beautiful garden.

It was very hot in summer and so houses were built with high ceilings because this helped the air to circulate. Rooms looked empty and cool because there was little furniture in them. Walls were plastered with different designs. Pieces of marble, shells or china were also used to decorate the walls.

Wood was painted in green, blue or other colours. Most people spent a lot of money on carpets and hangings for their houses. People sat cross-legged on hand-made carpets or on low platforms with cushions on them.

The most important piece of furniture in the room was the diwan or sofa which surrounded three sides of the room. Cushions were placed on small matrahs for people to sit on. The word mattress comes from the word matrah.

Food was served on large round brass trays set on a low table in front of the diwan. Everyone

1 a) Did rich or poor people live in the house shown in source A? Give reasons.
b) Do you think this house was a typical house or not? Use the text and the pictures to help you say why.
2 Did richer people live in houses built around courtyards just because they wanted peace and quiet? Give reasons.
3 a) If slaves were treated so well why didn't people try to become one?
b) What does the use of slaves tell you about Islamic society?
4 Compare a typical home today with the home described in this chapter. What are the differences and what are the similarities?

A A woman pounding grain, taken from an early 16th-century dictionary.

The Abbasid Arabs who conquered Iraq and founded Baghdad were dazzled by the brilliance of the people who lived there. They especially enjoyed eating their deliciously prepared food.

Arabs used ground almonds, walnuts and pistachio nuts to thicken sauces. Chickens were fed on milk and almonds to make them taste better. Sweet and sour dishes such as chicken and lemon, apricots and lamb were thought to be mouth-watering. Even eyes, brains, hearts and testicles were eaten.

At the end of Ramadan, the end of the fasting was celebrated with a great feast. At this time a whole lamb might be stuffed with fruits and almonds and seasoned with coriander and ginger.

Pork was never eaten because it was forbidden in the Qur'an. This was sensible because eating pork was a health hazard before refrigerators were invented.

Sherbet was drunk a lot. This was water sweetened with sugar and flavoured with violets, bananas and roses. Sometimes it was mixed with snow to make a long cool drink. Yogurt mixed with water was also drunk. The favourite drink was khamr which was made from dates. Although alcohol was forbidden in the Qur'an it was sometimes drunk.

Not everyone ate so well. Poorer people ate bread and vegetables, such as aubergines. Most people rarely ate meat except at festivals. It was only the wealthy who could afford such a varied diet.

B Edward William Lane, a 19th-century writer, described food eaten in the Middle Ages:

Among the more common dishes are the following: lamb or mutton, cut into small pieces, and stewed with various vegetables, and sometimes with peaches, apricots, and sugar; cucumbers, or aubergines stuffed with rice and minced meat, vine-leaves or pieces of lettuce-leaf or cabbage-leaf; small bits of lamb or mutton, roasted on skewers, and called kebab; fowls simply roasted or boiled, or boned and stuffed with raisins, pistachio-nuts, crumbled bread and parsley; and various kinds of pastry and other sweets.

The meal is frequently begun with soup; and is generally ended with boiled rice, mixed with a little butter and seasoned with salt and pepper; or after this is served, a water-melon or other fruit, or a bowl of a sweet drink composed of water with raisins and sometimes other kinds of fruit boiled in it, and then sugar, with a little rose-water added to it when cool.

---

1 Design a menu for people visiting you for dinner today. Include all the delicious food you can.
2 Design a menu as if you lived in Iraq in the Middle Ages.
3 What is the same and what is different about each menu? Explain the differences.
4 a) Do you think rich or poor people ate the food in source C? Give reasons for your answer.
   b) What can historians learn from recipe books?

D Eating and drinking at an inn (1237).

C A recipe using rose-water taken from a 13th-century collection of recipes by a gentleman gourmet called al-Baghdadi. It is a recipe for a 'makhfiya', meaning a simple dish.

Cut red meat into thin strips about four fingers long. Put the meat into the oil, with salt and finely ground dry coriander, and fry until browned. Then cover with water, adding green coriander leaves, cinnamon bark, a handful of peeled chick-peas and a handful of onion chopped fine. Bring to the boil, and remove the scum.

Now mince red meat fine and make into meatballs with seasonings. Take hard-boiled eggs; remove the whites and place the yolks in the middle of the meatballs; place them in the pot with the strips of meat. When almost cooked throw in fine-ground cumin and ginger. Take more eggs and beat well: remove the strips of meat, dip them while hot into the egg, and return to the pot.

Do this two or three times until the slices are well coated in egg. When the liquid in the pot has almost evaporated, sprinkle with finely powdered cumin and spray with rose-water. Leave to settle over a fire for an hour.

NON-MUSLIMS IN ISLAMIC LANDS

When Muhammad became ruler of Madinah there were many Jewish people living there. Muhammad wrote a set of rules, called a constitution, by which the country was governed. In the constitution, Muhammad stated that Jews and others were equal to Muslims. Jews were able to practise their own religion. So, too, were Christians.

Both Jews and Christians were thought to be 'People of the Book'. Muslims regarded the Torah of the Jews as a sacred book. The Christian Bible was also seen to be holy.

Muhammad was said to have been transported to Heaven at one point. There he met Jesus Christ and Abraham. He considered them to be important prophets.

Muslims did not force their own religion upon others. Jews and Christians were allowed to practise their faith in their synagogues and churches. However, they were forbidden to

A A 14th-century synagogue.

convert Muslims or to ring bells to advertise services. And they were not allowed to build new places of worship. Neither were they allowed to repair old ones unless they had permission.

Both Jews and Christians had to pay a poll tax which was called the jizya. This was little different from the alms tax every Muslim was supposed to pay. Because Muslims were not allowed to lend money, Christians and Jews became the early bankers. Muslims could inherit money and property from Christians and Jews. No Christian or Jew could inherit money from a Muslim.

The law favoured Muslims but Jews and Christians did not suffer from persecution. In many cities all three groups lived, studied and worked together in harmony. Jewish scholars were encouraged by the caliphs to study languages. They translated many Greek texts into Arabic. Some of the greatest achievements in science and medicine were as a result of joint work.

B This style of painting is called Mozarabic. It is a mixture of Muslim and Christian art.

Life was not always harmonious between these different religious groups. At times both Jews and Christians had to follow certain rules. In the ninth century, both had to wear different clothes from Muslims and to avoid wearing certain colours such as green because it was a colour associated with Muhammad. Instead they had to wear outer garments of yellow. Wooden images of devils had to be put outside their houses.

C This description of a caliph's behaviour comes from a book written by al-Maqrizi, an Egyptian scholar who lived in the 15th century.

In the year 1009 the Caliph, al-Hakim, ordered the Jews and Christians to wear sashes round their waists and distinguishing badges on their clothes.

He also forbade people to eat herbs and shellfish or to slaughter a healthy cow except for the feast of sacrifices. He forbade outright the sale and making of beer. He gave orders that women should not uncover their heads and that no fish without scales should be sold or caught by any fisherman.

In October 1009, al-Hakim wrote to Jerusalem ordering the destruction of the Church of the Holy Sepulchre.

In the year 1013 the Jews were compelled to wear bells round their necks when they entered the public baths. Al-Hakim ordered the Christians and the Jews to leave Egypt.

People's attitudes towards each other changed over time, but their religion remained the same. In looking at the causes for these differences in attitude historians have to look at other reasons as well as religion.

1 Look at sources A and B. What Islamic influences can you see?
2 Why did Muslims:
a) stop Christians and Jews wearing green?
b) make them put devils outside their houses?
c) stop new churches being built?
d) How do you think Christians and Jews felt about each of the above?
3 a) Do you think Muslims treated Christians and Jews fairly? Give reasons.
b) Do you think Christians and Jews thought they were being treated fairly? Again, give reasons.
4 Source C was written 400 years after the event it is describing.
a) What use is the source to a historian?
b) What questions might historians ask about this source?
5 Find out about how Christians treated Muslims and Jews in the land under their control. How does it differ from the treatment they received from the Muslims?

KEEPING HEALTHY

A Inside a bath house.

Islamic medicine is influenced by religion. Even today, personal hygiene, diet and washing are all important to Muslims worldwide. Islam requires its believers to wash themselves all the time so that they are clean for Allah.

Bath houses were often built to help Muslims keep pure and healthy. Doctors used the baths to cure headaches and other illnesses. A Muslim bath took several hours. First the body was washed, then rubbed with precious oils. Later, time was spent in the steam room and the cold room.

If people became ill they visited a doctor. Islamic doctors were more concerned with preventing illness rather than curing it. They made sure that their patients remained fit and well by eating properly.

Doctors were well thought of in the Muslim world. Many passed exams after training in special hospitals.

Caliphs employed doctors to keep them healthy and look after them when they fell sick. Doctors charged high fees from these wealthy patients. Poorer people were treated for free. Doctors even visited prisons. In some parts of Iraq doctors travelled by camel, carrying their precious medicines with them, in order to visit sick patients in the desert villages. These doctors would put up a tent in which they examined and treated their patients.

If patients were very ill they sometimes went to a hospital. All the founders of the hospitals were wealthy people such as caliphs. One story tells that the Caliph Mansur, who founded Baghdad, once had such terrible indigestion that no one could cure him. In desperation he asked the chief doctor in Iraq to visit him. This doctor was a Christian who had learnt his skill from Greek writings. When he succeeded in curing the caliph, interest in medicine grew.

Many Greek medical texts were translated into Arabic. In Europe this medical knowledge was lost. A doctor, called Hunayn, worked with his son, his nephew and 90 other people to translate these works as accurately as possible. Hunayn was paid the same weight in gold as the books he translated.

B An acupuncturist at work. Acupuncture began in China but was used in the Islamic empire.

C Dioscorides, a Greek doctor, with a student. Painted in Iraq in 1229.

D Ibn Batuta, a traveller (1306-1369) wrote:
The baths at Baghdad are numerous and well made, most of them being painted with pitch, which looks like black marble. Each establishment has a large number of private bathrooms. Every one has a wash-basin in the corner, with two taps supplying hot and cold water. Every bather is given three towels, one to wear round his waist when he comes out, and two to dry himself with. In no other town than Baghdad have I seen all this elaborate arrangement, though some other towns approach it in this respect.

E From *Hadith*, a book of the sayings of Muhammad:
Cleanliness is half of Faith. Keep your houses and yards tidy. God does not like dirt and untidiness. Brushing the teeth cleanses the mouth and pleases God. He who does not trim his nails and his moustache is not one of us. He who goes to sleep while his hands smell of food has only himself to blame if harm comes to him. Every Muslim must have a bath once a week, when he must wash his head and the whole of his body. Do not put up a sick man and a healthy one together.

F A reconstruction of an Islamic pharmacy.

Paintings can show something about the times in which the artist lived. They can teach the historian about the clothes, the architecture and work of the period. Historians can also find out about attitudes towards cleanliness by looking at paintings like the bath house. However, the historian should remember that artists give their own view of the scenes they draw.

1 a) Look at source A.
Describe what you see in all the numbered places.
The following list will help you:
- having a haircut
- preparing a bath
- drinking healthy liquid
- a servant bringing supplies
- water being drawn on a pulley by an ox

b) What can this source tell the historian about Islamic society?
c) What new information do you gain from reading this chapter? How do you think the writer might have got this information?

2 Look at sources B and C. What do these sources tell you about the spread of medical knowledge from one country to another?

3 Read source E. How did the Islamic religion help in the development of medicine?

SURGERY

Both Muslim and Christian doctors did not approve of surgery unless it could not be avoided. This was because they believed that the body of a dead person would rise again after death. This is called resurrection. If the body was cut up in different ways then it could not be resurrected.

Some operations might be carried out in emergencies. Muslim doctors operated on the brain and the stomach. Diseased arms and legs were sometimes cut off. This is called amputation. Caesarian operations were performed in difficult births. Doctors even operated for cancer, cutting out the diseased part. Injuries such as dislocated shoulders were put back into shape.

Ophthalmology was a highly developed skill. This is surgery on the eye. Doctors who practised ophthalmology were examined on their detailed knowledge of the eye. They had to know about all the different treatments which were possible.

Islamic doctors were very skilled in treating eye disease. Cataracts are defects in the lens of the eye which make it difficult for people to see properly. These were removed by using a tube to suck out the fluid. This method was used for centuries.

Some of the medical methods used seem a little strange to us today but they were sensible for the time. For instance, Muslims used red hot irons on a wound to help it heal. This was called cautery. One way to close a wound was to put ants on the edge of it and wait until they had bitten through the skin. Then they cut off the bottom half of the ant leaving the jaws fastened tightly.

When people were unfortunate enough to break a bone they were put in plaster. This was made from lime and white of egg which set just as hard as the plaster bandages of today.

Many of these operations were very painful. To avoid the patient screaming or fainting, opium was used to make them unconscious. The use of anaesthetics in English surgery was not really successful until the 19th century.

A Setting a dislocated shoulder.

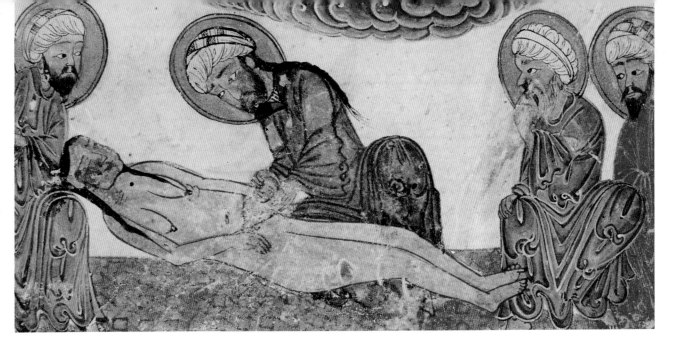

B A caesarian operation.

C Usana ibn-munqidh, an Arab writer of the Middle Ages:

One day, a Frankish governor wrote to my uncle the Sultan, asking him to send a physician to treat several urgent cases.

My uncle selected one of our doctors, a man named Thabit. He was gone for just a few days, and then returned home. We were all very curious to know how he had been able to cure the patients so quickly, and we besieged him with questions. Thabit answered: 'They brought before me a knight who had an abscess on his leg and a woman suffering from consumption . I made a plaster for the knight, and the swelling opened and improved. For the woman I prescribed a diet.

'Then a Christian doctor arrived and objected, "This man does not know how to care for them." And, addressing the knight, he asked him, "Which do you prefer, to live with one leg or die with two?"

'When the patient answered that he preferred to live with just one leg, the physician ordered, "Bring me a strong knight with a well-sharpened battleaxe".

'The knight and the axe soon arrived. The Frankish doctor placed the man's leg on a chopping block, telling the new arrival, "Strike a sharp blow to cut cleanly." Before my very eyes, the man struck an initial blow, but then, since the leg was still attached, he struck a second time. The marrow of the leg spurted out and the wounded man died that very instant. As for the woman, the Christian doctor examined her and said, "She has an evil spirit in her head who has fallen in love with her. Cut her hair!"

'They cut her hair. The woman then began to eat her food again, with its garlic and mustard, which made her worse. Their doctor said, "The devil himself must have entered her head." Then, grasping a razor, he cut an incision in the shape of a cross, exposed the bone of the skull, and rubbed it with salt. The woman died on the spot.

'I then asked, "Have you any further need of me?" They said no, and I returned home, having learned much that I had never known about the medicine of the Christian.'

Sources are often biased. Two people may see the same event in different ways. Even if the writer is biased the source can still be useful. For instance, it may tell us what different groups of people thought at the time.

1 a) According to the text, why do you think many Muslims were against surgery?
b) What extra reason does source C offer?
c) What can source C tell the historian about
i) how Muslims treated their patients and
ii) how Christians treated their patients?

2 a) Source C is written from a Muslim point of view. How might a Christian doctor tell the same story?
b) If your description of what the Christian doctor might have said is so different from the Muslim point of view, what can that tell us about the reliability of historical sources?
c) If source C is unreliable is it of any use?

3 Look at source B.
a) How safe do you think this operation is? Think about germs, surgical instruments, anaesthetics and antiseptics to help you answer.
b) What improvements do you think could be made to make the operation safer?

FAMOUS DOCTORS

Al-Rhazi

Al-Rhazi, who is known as Rhazes in the West, lived between 865-925. He was one of the greatest doctors of all time. A Muslim who was born in Persia, Al-Rhazi worked as a singer until he was 30, then went to study medicine in Baghdad.

When the caliph, al-Mansur, wanted to build a hospital in Baghdad, he consulted Al-Rhazi. It was built with great care. To make sure that he chose the healthiest site, Al-Rhazi is said to have hung up shreds of meat in different places. He then chose the spot where the meat was the least rotten.

Al-Rhazi was later was put in charge of Baghdad hospital. Every patient was observed very carefully. This hospital held about 8,000 people. There were separate wards for men and women, for fevers, dysentery and surgery. People were employed to clean the wards and look after the sick. Inside the hospital were lecture halls, a library and even a mosque. This hospital at Baghdad became the centre for Islamic medicine. It was copied all over the Muslim world.

One of his books, *Al Hawi*, was an encyclopaedia of all medical science up to that time. For every disease, Al-Rhazi gave the opinions of Greek, Syrian, Hindu and Persian writers. He also added his own opinion. It was thought so important that it was translated into Latin in 1279 by a Jewish doctor called Caraj ibn Salim. Altogether Al-Rhazi wrote about 100 other books on medicine.

One of Al-Rhazi's books was the first to describe the symptoms of smallpox. This meant that doctors in the future were able to diagnose and treat patients who contracted this disease. Al-Rhazi's treatment for smallpox patients was used for hundreds of years. His advice was sensible. Each smallpox patient was to rest, eat sensibly and live in clean surroundings.

Ibn Sina

B A 15th-century European woodcut of Ibn Sina.

Another famous doctor was Ibn Sina who was known as Avicenna in the West. Ibn Sina was also Persian and lived from 980 to 1037. Like Al-Rhazi he wrote many books about medicine. He was so clever that he had learnt the Qur'an off by heart when he was ten. By the time he was 18 he had become a personal doctor to a Sultan.

A Woodcut portrait of Al-Rhazi, date unknown.

Ibn Sina wrote the Canon of Medicine which dealt with the treatment of different diseases. In this book Ibn Sina recognised that tuberculosis was contagious and that certain diseases can be spread by water. His work was considered so important that it was translated into Latin. The Canon of Medicine was used more widely than the works of Galen and Hippocrates, two famous Greek doctors. This book was studied in Europe from the 12th to the 17th century.

POSTAGE

HAKIM IBN-E-SINA (980-1037)

HEALTH FROM HERBS

C An artist's impression of a 20th-century stamp of Ibn Sina.

D Ibn Sina (980-1037) wrote:

By studying the irregularities of the pulse it may be possible to discover the identity of a loved one, if the patient will not reveal it. This is done by repeating any names while keeping the finger on the pulse. When it becomes very irregular and almost ceases, one should repeat the process. I have tried this method many times and have discovered the name of the loved one.

In the same way, mention the streets, homes, arts, families and countries, joining each one with the name of the loved one. All the time feel the pulse. When it alters on the mention of any one thing several times, you will be able to find out the name, appearance and job of the loved one.

Sources can tell historians more about the time in which they were drawn or written than the event they show.

Some historians argue that some individuals have caused things to happen in the past. Life would be very different without them. For example, some historians would argue that without Al-Rhazi, Arab medicine would not have developed.

Others argue that individuals aren't that important. They would argue that even if Al-Rhazi had never been born, Arabic medicine would still have improved.

E A 15th-century Hebrew translation of Ibn Sina's Canon of Medicine.

1   Look at sources B and C.
   a) What is different about these sources?
   b) Why do you think these sources are so different?
   c) If these sources are so different, can either of them be of any value? Explain your answer.

2   a) Look at source E.
   What can this source tell you about Islamic medicine? You might like to consider hygiene, the chemist's shop, the use of surgery in your answer.
   b) What can this source tell you about the spread of Islamic knowledge?

3   a) Does your pulse rate change when you are frightened or excited?
   b) Do you think there is any truth in the claims Ibn Sina makes in source D? Explain your answer.

4   What part did Al-Rhazi play in the development of medicine?

SCIENCE AND TECHNOLOGY

ASTRONOMY

Scientists were very interested in the study of the stars and planets. This is called astronomy. Travellers use the position of the stars to work out which way they should go. The position of the stars can also be used to find the direction of Makkah.

Knowledge of astronomy was brought to Baghdad in about 771 from India. Al-Mahmun, Caliph of Baghdad, built an observatory to study the stars. A Jewish person called Sind ibm-Ali, who had become a Muslim, was in charge of it. Regular observations were made of the movements of the moon and other planets. Astronomers used their knowledge of mathematics to help them.

Astronomers used different equipment such as the quadrant, globe and astrolabe to help them in their work. Some of these had been invented by people in other countries.

B Europeans studying a Muslim book.

A A modern astrolabe maker in Isfahan.

Greeks used astrolabes before the Muslims. They looked like flat discs. Brass was usually used to make them. Astrolabes could be very small or very large. Some were only 5 cms across whereas others were over 30 cms across.

Astrolabes were used by travellers and traders to find their way. By using astrolabes to measure the distance of the sun and the stars, people could work out where they were. These instruments were used to tell the time, measure the height of mountains and the depth of wells. Scientists even managed to work out the size of the earth from them. They realised that the earth was round. Many Europeans still believed that the earth was flat.

Astrolabes were very useful devices. Explorers were able to cross seas, oceans and unknown lands with the use of astrolabes. They were used by travellers until the 18th century.

Most of the astronomers also studied astrology, which is a study of the stars and planets to tell the future. Today it is no longer regarded as a science but many people still consult their stars in newspapers and magazines. Most people know their own star sign. Do you?

Both Muslims and Christians thought astrology and astronomy were equally important. Rulers and ordinary people alike consulted their stars before they did anything important.

C   Astronomers at work.

1   Look at source C.
a) Name the numbered instruments using the following to help you: compass, globe, astrolabe, sand-timer, quadrant.
b) Describe what these instruments were used for.
c) Why were these instruments important to astronomers?
d) What else can this source tell us about astronomy at this time?

2   Look at source B. What can this source tell the historian about the spread of Islamic science?
3   a) Look at source A. Why do you think astrolabes are still made?
b) Why are they no longer used in your maths and geography lessons? Give reasons why they are no longer used.

MATHEMATICS

Numerals.

Roman	Today	Arabic
1	1	1
11	2	2
111	3	3
1V	4	5
V	5	4
V1	6	6
V11	7	7
V111	8	8
1X	9	9
X	10	0
XIV	14	1⌐
XX	20	20

When you add up how much pocket money you have left to spend you are using a system based on Arabic numbers. Our decimal system and the use of zero also came from this part of the world. This number system originally came from the Hindus in India but was made popular, in Europe, by the Arabs. Western Europe used Roman numerals in the Middle Ages which made maths very difficult.

A son of an Italian trader, called Leonardo Fibonacci, brought the Arabic numerals to Europe. He lived from 1180-1250. We can see his influence in the word zero. Islamic mathematicians used a dot or small circle for zero. The word for this was sifr which was translated into Italian as zero.

Although the Arabic numerals were easier than the Roman ones many people would not use them at first. By the end of the Middle Ages most people in Europe recognised that these new numbers were much easier for adding up.

Mathematicians also enjoyed making magic squares. This meant that each line of numbers always added up to the same number whichever way you looked.

When you study algebra in your maths lesson you are also using an Arab technique. Al-Khwarizmi, known as Algorismus, worked out the algebra system. It was called Al-jabr. (Say it out loud!) Al-Khwarizmi's book was translated into Latin in the 12th century.

B Magic squares.

16	2	3	13
5	11	10	8
9	7	6	12
4	14	15	1

A four row magic square

4		8
9		1
	7	6

A three row magic square. Each line adds up to 15.

Technology

The Muslims used their knowledge of science and mathematics to help solve everyday problems. One of these was getting enough water to the towns and to the farm lands. They developed many systems.

C

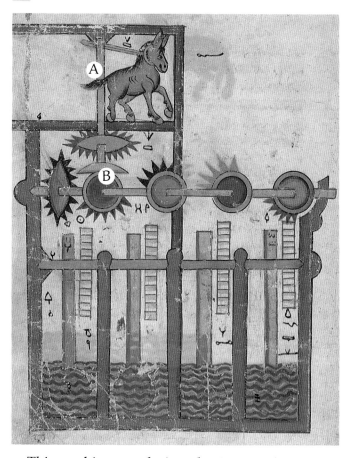

This machine was designed to irrigate the land. It was invented in northern Iraq by the engineer Jazari in the 13th century. As the donkey walks round, it turns the upright pole (A). This pole then moves a set of geared wheels (B) which are linked to four water scoops. By turning the wheels, the contents of each scoop are emptied into the canal.

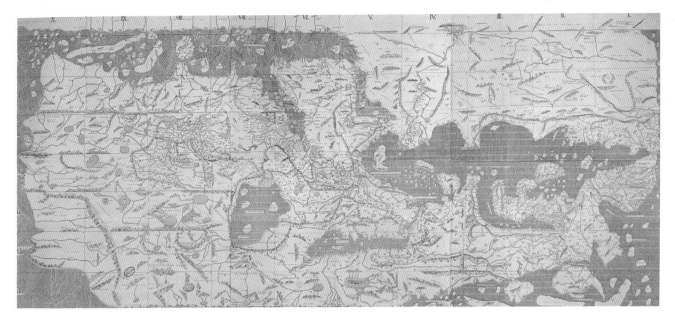

D Mappa Arabaciae, drawn in 1154, showing Europe, North Africa and the Middle East. The lakes are painted in green and the seas are in blue.

E These water wheels are on the river Orontes in Syria. They were built in the 12th century. The running river water forces the wheels to turn round. As it does so, its paddles scoop water up into an aqueduct and the water is carried away to irrigate the fields.

1 a) Look at source A. Write down the sum 3 + 4 + 7 in both Roman and Arabic numerals. Now work it out.
b) If Roman numerals were so difficult to add up why did people keep using them?

2 Look at source B.
a) Add up the numbers across, the numbers down and the numbers diagonally. What answer do you get?
b) Work out the missing numbers in the 3 line magic square.

3 a) In pairs, think of as many ways you can to move water from one place to another. Then write them in your book.
b) What problems, if any, would you meet in moving water from place to place?

4 Look carefully at source D. It shows the areas of the world known to the Arabs at that time. If you turn the map upside down it is easier to recognise the areas on the map.
a) Using a modern atlas to help you, find Saudi Arabia, Italy, Spain, England and Egypt.
b) Write down the names of three big countries that are known to us today which are not shown on this map.
c) Why do you think they are not shown?

5 'Muslim scientists merely copied other people.' Say why you agree or disagree with this statement and explain why.

Many people believe Muslims are not allowed to draw or paint human beings or animals.

In fact, this idea did not begin until the 8th century, almost 100 years after the Hijra. In 721 the Caliph Yazid ordered all the paintings and statues of people or animals to be destroyed.

Islamic art has been influenced by this idea that it is wrong to paint living beings. No mosque in the world today has pictures of people or animals in it. All the designs are   abstract   .

Even so, in palaces and the private homes of the wealthy, particularly in countries such as Iran, Iraq, India and Turkey, people and animals are shown in paintings, statues and pottery.

Most people, however, preferred not to have paintings of living beings. As a result, flowers and vegetables became very popular decorations. Tulips, roses, cherry, lotus and almond blossoms were especially liked. Leaves, cloud scrolls and waves were also used in designs. So was calligraphy.

Calligraphy is the art of beautiful writing. Pottery, trays, carpets, textiles and mosques were all decorated by calligraphers.

To write in Arabic was thought to be most holy because Muhammad had received the word of God in this language. Calligraphers were very important people because they wrote the language of God. They became much more famous than painters.

A lot of this wonderful art has disappeared so we can only imagine what some of the treasures of the great palaces were like. In the reign of al-Mustansir (1036-94) the treasure of the Fatimids was stolen. Great amounts of treasure went missing. It included:

- pearls and jewels
- crowns and swords
- eighteen thousand pieces of rock crystal and cut glass
- thirty-six thousand pieces of jewellery
- gold and silver knives
- six thousand gilded silver scent bottles
- gold animals inset with jewels

It must have been a magnificent collection, worth a great deal of money.

This is what some people have said about painting human beings and animals.

A 'The Qur'an forbids pictures of living beings. It says that ". . . wine, games of chance, statues, (al-Ansab) are a crime, and come from the devil!"'

B 'God is the only creator. When humans draw or paint living things they are competing with God.'

C 'When you make drawings of humans you are making idols. Muhammad forbade the worship of idols.'

D 'In the Qur'an, the word al-ansab is translated as statues. Al-ansab really means idol.'

E 'Muhammad did not approve of human drawings. Remember the time when he arrived home and found Ai'shah with a cushion with pictures on it. Muhammad refused to enter the house because angels refuse to go into a home with pictures of living beings in it.'

F 'When Muhammad visited the Ka'abah he destroyed 360 idols.'

G 'Hadith or the traditions prohibit pictures of people or animals, not the Qur'an.'

1   Read sources A-G. Draw up a list and put all the sources which agree that living beings can be shown in art in group A and those which disagree in group B.
b) Make up an argument against either group A or group B to convince the writers that they are wrong.

2   a) Using the text to help you, write down all the different motifs you can see in source I.
b) Design a plate using some of the different motifs shown in source H.

H Some designs used by Islamic potters.

I A pottery dish. Pottery called 'lustre' was invented in Persia in the 9th century.

J Carpets were thought to be great luxuries and were woven from wool and silk. Europeans copied the idea in about the 14th century. In the 16th century, Cardinal Wolsey once ordered 60 carpets from the Arabs to use at Hampton Court.

3 Which of the objects on this page would not be used by a religious person. Why?
4 Why has Islamic art remained unchanged for so many years?
5 What can Islamic art tell you about the society in which it was created?

EDUCATION

Girls and boys were educated differently. Boys went to a school which was attached to a mosque when they were six years old. They were not allowed to be taught inside the mosque in case they damaged anything. Boys were taught to read and write by studying the Qur'an. Each day the teacher read out parts of the Qur'an which the boys wrote on a tablet.

A A mosque school (1237).

Learning the facts off by heart was considered to be important. Boys were expected to learn the Qur'an word for word. They were often allowed a holiday when they had learnt a whole section of the holy book. In Baghdad children were paraded on camels so that everyone could see how clever they were.

If any pupil was naughty they were punished. One punishment involved the child lying on his back on the floor. Assistants held up his legs whilst his feet were beaten with palms by the teacher.

Wealthy boys were taught privately. They also learnt how to read, write and to recite the Qur'an from memory. When they were older they studied and wrote poetry. It was thought to be clever to be able to quote from poems. Many young men found it as easy to speak in verse as to speak in prose.

Nearly every mosque had schools for older students. These were called madrasahs. The students sat in a circle round a teacher and asked questions. Each mosque usually had a library containing text books and reference works. Some libraries had cubicles where the pupils could study.

When a student had finished studying a book with a teacher he received a certificate. This was called an ijaza. Some clever students travelled long distances to follow the lectures of the famous teachers. These students often collected many ijazas for all the books they had read.

Girls were allowed to study but not many parents let them. Only a few were taught to read. Most girls were taught at home by their mothers. They learnt how to spin and sometimes how to weave. Richer girls were taught embroidery. Mothers taught their daughters parts of the Qur'an which they were expected to learn.

B Al-Rashid (who died in 1318) wrote to the tutor of his son al-Amin:

Don't be too strict because it might stop him learning. Don't be too lenient because he might become lazy. Teach him through kindness and gentleness but if that doesn't work be severe and use force.

C Edward William Lane, a 19th-century author, wrote this about education in Persia in the Middle Ages:

There was reading in the morning but writing took up the rest of the day, with some breaks. Tuesday afternoon and Thursday morning were set aside for revision of what had been learnt. Friday was a holiday . . .

School fees were added up either monthly or annually. The curriculum was divided into two sections; one included the teaching of the Qur'an, religious instruction, reading and writing; and one which included pre-Islamic history, the history of the Prophet and his companions, poetry, grammar, composition, vocabulary, arithmetic and calligraphy.

Few of the children receive much instruction in literature, and still fewer are taught even the basics of any of the sciences; but there are numerous schools in their towns, and one at least in almost every large village. The former are mostly attached to mosques and other public buildings, and are paid for by princes or other men of rank, or wealthy tradesmen. In these the children are taught either free or for a very small weekly payment.

D Students with their teacher (1237).

1 Why do you think there was such an emphasis on religious education?

2 a) What was the attitude of people in Baghdad to the education of boys and girls?

b) Why do historians find out about how children were educated in the past?

c) What can this tell them about the society they are studying?

3 Compare Islamic education with your education. What, if any, are the differences in: (a) who attends; (b) the curriculum; (c) discipline and (d) teachers?

Day after day most people worked hard to earn a living. There was little time left for leisure. A lucky few had time to enjoy themselves.

Polo, hunting, chess, wrestling and archery were all popular pastimes. Children played with dolls, spinning tops and yoyos. They also used hobby horses and swings. Everyone liked music and stories. Poets and story-tellers were well respected in the Islamic court. Caliphs loved listening to poets reciting their work.

A Shirin and Khusraw listening to stories.

Sometimes poets spoke about sport. A famous poem about the Iranian ruler Khusraw Parviz and the Armenian princess, Shirin, tells of their romance. The poet writes about the polo match they played and the hunting they both enjoyed.

B Swinging.

In one poem, Khusraw put on a crown, earrings and a tunic made from gold to go hunting. He took 300 horses and 1,000 men with him. There were also 700 falconers with royal falcons and hawks, 300 keepers of cheetahs, 70 leopards and lions all wearing brocade and gold muzzles. Minstrels on camels played harps for the hunters whilst slaves burnt incense to make the air smell sweet.

The Arabian Nights

Story-telling was another popular pastime. The most famous of all the stories were *The Arabian Nights*. These began to take shape during the time of Harun al-Rashid between 786 and 809, even though *The Arabian Nights* were not finished until the 14th and 15th centuries.

It is said, in one of the stories, that these tales were told by Shahrazad. She was a young woman who had just married a king who murdered his wives the morning after the wedding. To save her life Shahrazad kept the king entertained by her lively stories.

These stories lasted for a thousand and one nights. During this time she had three sons. Shahrazad managed to persuade the king not to kill her because her children would be without a mother.

C Playing with dolls.

1 Look at sources A, B and C. What can these pictures tell the historian about aspects of life, other than leisure, at this time? You might want to consider the role of men and women, lighting, clothes, furniture, architecture.

2 Look at the pictures of children playing.
   a) Are these games still played today?
   b) What can that tell us about change and continuity?

How people spend their free time tells historians a lot about the way people live. In Britain today it is not only the wealthy who can afford to have leisure. Most people have the time and money to enjoy themselves. Some play or watch sport like tennis, football or hockey. Swimming and cycling are popular. Others visit cinemas and theatres to see films and plays. Many people spend a lot of their spare time watching television or playing video games. These leisure activities show that people do not have to work every single hour of the day, that technology is sophisticated, that spectators travel long distances to watch their favourite sport. They can also tell us about people's health.

ALADDIN AND THE LAMP

One story that Shahrazad told was of Aladdin and the magic lamp. This is it.

Once upon a time, a long time ago, in a large city far away there lived a poor tailor called Mustapha. This poor tailor lived with his wife and a good-for-nothing son called Aladdin. Nothing could be done for this boy.

Despite threats and beatings all Aladdin wanted to do was to be with his mates. Mustapha was in despair. Aladdin's behaviour led Mustapha to an early death, leaving Aladdin's mother alone in the world. This made Aladdin behave even more badly. Only when he was desperately hungry and exhausted from lack of sleep would Aladdin return home. His poor mother did not know what to do.

One fine day, when Aladdin was up to no good with his friends, a stranger dressed in fine clothes and wearing expensive jewellery spoke to him excitedly and hugged him. Aladdin thought he was a raving lunatic. But the stranger gave Aladdin lots of money, promised him all the presents he wanted and said that he was Aladdin's uncle. Aladdin didn't care much who the stranger was but took the money anyway. The stranger arranged with Aladdin to meet his mother the next day.

For the first time in his life Aladdin stayed at home that morning, waiting for the stranger. His mother was very suspicious. She feared the worst. When the stranger arrived he was carrying lots of presents. Aladdin's mother was won over by his charm and good manners. She invited him for tea.

The stranger accepted. Everyone sat down to enjoy a good old gossip about the past. The stranger was alarmed that Aladdin could not read or write properly, and had no job and little money. He promised to buy Aladdin a shop of his own so that he could make his own living.

Aladdin looked far too untidy to work in a shop selling cloth. He looked so scruffy and bedraggled that the stranger took him out shopping. Purchasing only the best that money could buy, the stranger clothed Aladdin in all the finest designer gear. Aladdin looked splendid. None of his friends recognised him on the streets.

The next day the stranger took Aladdin out again. This time they left the town to see the countryside. Aladdin did not like the countryside very much: it was too quiet and lonely. No one was around. The only sound to be heard was the song of the birds and the whistling of the wind.

Suddenly the stranger stopped. Darkness fell, thunder clapped and lightning flashed as the ground opened before them. A slab of stone appeared with a brass ring attached to it.

All of this frightened Aladdin. He wanted to run away, but was roughly stopped by the stranger. Aladdin was ordered to lift the stone and go inside. He had no choice but to obey.

'Dear nephew,' said the stranger, now all sweetness and light, 'climb down the steps until you reach the bottom. There you will find an unlocked door which leads into a vault. This vault has three rooms. In each room there will be bronze vases filled to the brim with gold and silver. Do not touch the vases or you will die.

'Walk through the rooms without stopping for a moment, until you reach a garden. Cross the garden until you see a lamp which is burning bright. Pick up the light, put it out, pour the oil away and bring it to me.'

With these instructions, the stranger smiled and gave Aladdin an expensive-looking ring. This made Aladdin more cheerful. He liked the way the ring's brightly-coloured stones glistened in the sunlight.

For once in his life, Aladdin did as he was told. Although he was frightened by the dark and gloomy cave, he climbed inside. Aladdin whistled loudly to scare away any evil spirits and did not stop walking until he reached the cave which held the lamp. This place was magnificent. The lamp was in the prettiest garden he had ever seen. It was hard to understand why his uncle wanted such a dull old item when there was so much beauty around.

By this time Aladdin was starving so on the way back he picked some of the fruit on the trees in the garden. But the fruit was as hard as rock. It was made of coloured stones that Aladdin could not eat.

He was very disappointed. But he put the stones into his pocket because he liked all their different colours shining in the bright sunshine of the garden. Aladdin did not know they were precious stones like diamonds, rubies and pearls.

When he returned to the entrance of the cave, the stranger asked Aladdin for the lamp. Aladdin, who always liked to tease, refused. So the stranger, who was very angry with this silly little boy, mumbled a few words. Instantly the slab of stone closed over the entrance, leaving Aladdin in total darkness.

For days and for nights Aladdin sat by himself in the cave. First he cried, then he slept, then he prayed to Allah. In his misery he rubbed the ring.

In a flash of lightning a spirit appeared and asked Aladdin's wish. The boy's greatest desire at that moment was to be outside the cave. His wish was granted at once and Aladdin found himself in the bright sunshine once more.

Running home as fast as his wicked legs could carry him, Aladdin told his story to his mother. His mother was used to all of Aladdin's lying and scheming, so she would not believe his adventures. Instead she thought Aladdin had been out with his friends for longer than usual. And as usual he had been up to no good. And as usual he had only come home when he was hungry.

This time there was no food in the house and no money to buy any. It looked as if Aladdin and his mother would starve to death. So Aladdin decided to sell the lamp that he had found in the cave. It would not be worth very much, but cleaned up a little it might fetch enough money for a meal.

For once in his life Aladdin set to work. Soon he had rubbed all the dirt off the lamp. Before he could say 'Salman Saladin' a genie appeared. By now, Aladdin was used to such strange events. He greeted the spirit calmly and coolly.

1 Finish the story of Aladdin in your own words.
2 a) This story was written in 1993. It is based on *The Arabian Nights*. How can you tell that it has been rewritten?
   b) How can you tell that it is a Muslim story?
3 Write or act out this story as a play. Each group should take one scene and develop it. Use the following to help you: at home, meeting with a stranger, new clothes, in the cave, Aladdin freed, your story.

WARS WITH THE CHRISTIANS

500	600	700	800	900	1000	1100	1200	1300	1400	1500	1600

In 1096, a series of wars between Muslims and Christians started in Syria and Palestine. These wars lasted on and off for over 300 years. The Muslims call them the 'Frankish Wars'. Western historians call these wars the 'Crusades'.

For Western Christians, these wars were a major event. Kings, knights, priests, nuns, peasants and even children went to fight in them. They came mainly from France, Italy and Germany. Those who stayed at home had to pay extra taxes to pay for the wars.

The Muslims did not think these wars were so important. As you can see from the map, fighting only happened on the edges of the Islamic empire. The Muslim historian, Ibn Khaldun, included only a couple of paragraphs about the Crusades in his book written during the Middle Ages. When the Christians marched into Syria and Palestine, they did not threaten the centres of Muslim power like Baghdad or Makkah. But they *did* threaten Jerusalem.

Why did the fighting start?

Historians try to work out why events happened in the past. They try to find out the causes. Events in the past usually have more than one cause.

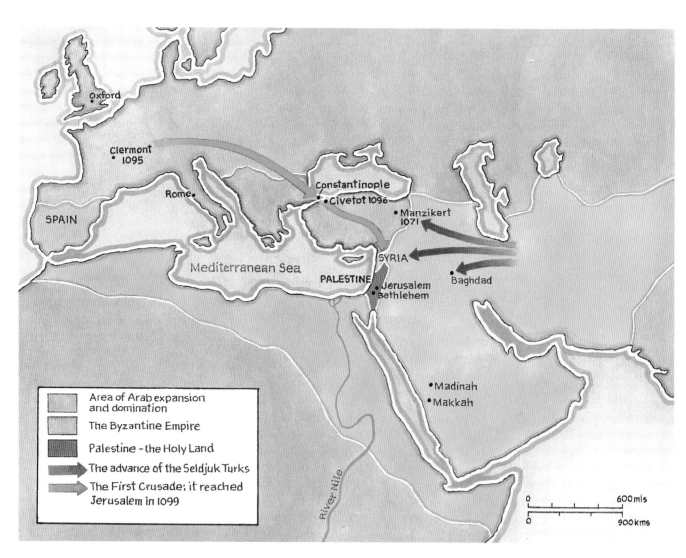

A Map showing events and places mentioned in this chapter.

B This is from a mosaic, showing the Madaba map of Jerusalem.

Jerusalem was a holy city for Jews, Christians and Muslims. Pilgrims from all three religions visited the holy sights. Muslims went to the Dome of the Rock, Jews to the Wailing Wall and Christians to the Holy Sepulchre where Christ's body had been laid.

Jerusalem had been captured by the Muslims in 637. At first this did not cause problems for the Christians. Then, in 1009, the Caliph of Egypt, al-Hakim, destroyed the Church of the Holy Sepulchre, and Jews and Christians were persecuted.

Al-Hakim did not just attack Jerusalem, he also tried to change the way people lived their lives.

C Al-Maqrizi, a 15th-century Egyptian scholar:
Several taxes were abolished, music and games were forbidden, as also were the sale of singing girls and pleasure parties in the desert.

D Al-Maqrizi also wrote about al-Hakim in the 15th century.
On 4 October, al-Hakim wrote to Jerusalem ordering the church of the Holy Sepulchre be pulled down. He also established a new register office to register property seized from executed people. He destroyed the monastery known as Dayr al-Qasr and made Christians and Jews wear a special mark. He forbade people to sail on the canal on boats and had doors and windows of houses overlooking the canal blocked up.

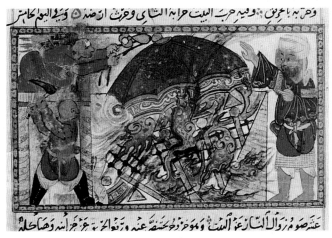

E Al-Hakim orders the destruction of the Holy Sepulchre. From a 14th-century Persian manuscript.

The Seldjuk Turks

In 1055, the Seldjuk Turks became very powerful. The Muslims called these powerful rulers Sultans. Their armies captured Baghdad as well as Syria and Iran. In 1071, they defeated the Eastern Christian army at Manzikert as they moved west towards Europe. By 1076, they had taken over Jerusalem and most of Palestine.

1. a) Why do you think the Muslims and the Christians saw these wars differently?
   b) From the information you have been given here, work out why the Christians went to fight against the Muslims.
2. a) Sources D and E are about the same event. Make a list in your book saying what each one tell you about Muslim society in 1009.
   b) How would our understanding of al-Hakim be different without source D?
   c) Both sources were produced after the events they describe. Work out how long.
   d) Make a list of the questions historians need to ask of these two sources.

WERE THERE OTHER REASONS FOR THE WARS?

Pilgrimages to Jerusalem

The life of Christians in Jerusalem under the Seldjuk Turks was better than it had been under al-Hakim. However, it was very difficult for Christians from Europe to travel there. From Constantinople onwards, pilgrims needed an armed escort. The road was full of dangers. Robbers attacked the travellers at every opportunity. Local lords taxed them. When they at last got back to Europe, they told their tales of misery and how hard their journey had been.

Alexius I – Emperor of Constantinople

He became the new leader of the Byzantine empire and Head of the Orthodox Church in 1081. His capital city, Constantinople, was said to be the richest city in the world. Many scholars lived there and learning was very important. Alexius had over 4,000 books in his library. At the same time, the king of England had only nine books!

In 1081, Alexius had to swallow his pride and ask his old enemies, the Western Christians, for help.

A The Emperor Alexius I of Constantinople. When he became emperor his empire was surrounded by enemies. He ruled for 37 years.

B From the monk Bernold of Constance (about 1100). Bernold wanted closer links between the Church in Rome and the Church in Constantinople.

A messenger came from the emperor of Constantinople to the Pope. He humbly begged him and all who followed Christ to send him help for the defence of the church against the   pagans . For these pagans were then attacking these parts and had conquered all the lands up to the walls of Constantinople.

The Pope

For about 500 years, the Christians, led by the Pope in Rome, had tried to bring themselves and the Orthodox Christians together. So when Alexius asked for help in 1081, Pope Urban II saw his chance. In 1095, at Clermont, he called all men to promise to save the Holy Land before it was too late.

C Urban II preaching at Clermont. He is calling on all men to swear to take up the sword and fight the Muslims to defend Jerusalem. From a French 15th-century manuscript.

D One of the Crusaders, Baldwin I, captured the kingdom in Edessa from the Muslims in 1098. Here the citizens of Edessa are swearing an oath to Baldwin to say they accept him as their king. From a manuscript written by William of Tyre who wrote a history of the Crusades in 1173.

E From a letter written by St Bernard of Clairvaux in 1140.

Oh mighty soldier, oh man of war, you now have something to fight for. If you win it will be glorious. If you die fighting for Jerusalem you will win a place in heaven.

Or are you a shrewd businessman, a man quick to see the profits of this world? If you are, I can offer you a splendid bargain. Do not miss this opportunity. Take the sign of the cross and at once you will have forgiveness for the sins which you confess.

F From a history book, *The Clash of Cultures* by Brian Catchpole (1981).

One of the problems in the 1090's was that good land was in short supply. Younger sons simply had no land. Their 'land-hunger' caused constant warfare among the warrior class. For many, a crusade seemed an instant solution to a pressing problem. They could fight for the cross and for personal profit also.

G From a history book, *The Influence of Islam on Medieval Europe* by W. Montgomery Watt (1972)

For centuries, Islam had been the great enemy, controlling the Mediterranean from Spain to Syria. Even after 1100 western Europeans still thought that the Muslims occupied more than half of the world. Many were also aware of the cultural superiority of the Arabs.

Historians try to find out why people acted as they did in the past. In other words, they try to find out the motives for people's actions. People often have more than one motive for acting in the way they do. Historians try to find out these motives, such as why knights went to fight in the Crusades.

1 a) Draw a chart in your book. You will need six columns, so draw your chart across a double page. Put the following headings at the top of the columns: Motives, Fame and Fortune, Religious, Economic , Political, Adventure.

b) In the MOTIVES column write *The Pope*. Explain what his motives were for becoming involved in the Crusades. Use the headings at the top of each column to help you. For example, if you think the Pope had political motives, write what you think they were in the column headed *Political*.

c) Do the same for each column. You may not think the Pope had all five motives. If, for example, you do not think the Pope became involved in the Crusades from motives of adventure, then leave that column blank.

d) Do the same, in turn, for: the Seldjuk Turks (Muslims), Alexius I and the medieval knights.

e) Which do you think were the Muslims' most important motives for fighting? Explain your answer.

f) Which do you think were the Christians' most important motives for fighting? Explain your answer.

16

THE CRUSADERS: INVADERS OR HEROES?

500	600	700	800	900	1000	1100	1200	1300	1400	1500	1600

In 1096, thousands of people who were not trained fighters or soldiers trailed across Europe on the difficult journey towards the Holy Land. They had set off ahead of the organised army of Christian princes. This Crusade is known as The People's Crusade. It was led by Peter the Hermit.

A Anna Comnena was the daughter of Alexius I. In 1139, 40 years after the First Crusade, she wrote a history of her father's rule. She described what happened to this People's Crusade:

They fell into the Turkish ambushes and were miserably wiped out. Large numbers of Franks were killed by the Turks. When the remains of the slaughtered men were collected, they did not only make a mound or peak, but a huge mountain, deep and wide, most remarkable, so great was the pile of bones.

Some men of the same race as these Crusaders, later when they were building a large wall, used the bones of the dead as pebbles to fill up the gaps.

B Peter the Hermit at the head of the Crusades. From a 14th-century manuscript.

The Crusaders who followed were much more organised. In 1097-8 they occupied parts of Palestine, and by 1099 were ready to march to capture Jerusalem.

People see events that happened in the past differently. The Crusaders and the Muslims saw the wars in a different way. The historian has to understand why people hold these different points of view and what their strengths and weaknesses are.

C From Ibn al-Athir. He was a historian who lived from 1160-1233.

The population of the city was put to the sword and the Franks spent a week massacring the Muslims. They killed more than seventy thousand people in the al-Aqsa mosque.

D Ibn al-Qalanisi, historian (1073-1160).

Many people were killed. The Jews had gathered in their synagogue and the Franks burned them alive. They also destroyed the monuments of saints and the tomb of Abraham, may peace be upon him.

E The *Gesta Francorum*, written by an unknown crusader on the First Crusade. He was at the siege of Jerusalem when it fell on 15 July 1099.

Our pilgrims entered the city, and chased the Saracens, killing as they went as far as the Temple of Solomon. There the enemy assembled and fought a furious battle for the whole day, so that their blood flowed all over the Temple. At last the pagans were overcome, and our men captured a good many men and women in the Temple; they killed who they wished, and chose to keep others alive.

Soon our army overran the whole city, seizing gold and silver, horses and mules and houses full of riches of all kinds.

In 1176, the great Sultan Saladin began to push the Crusaders out of the Holy Land. In September 1187, Saladin recaptured Jerusalem.

F Imad ad-Din, Saladin's secretary, wrote an account of Saladin's life in about 1193.

The Muslims took possession of the city on Friday 2 October 1187, just at the time when the Friday prayers were due. Saladin's flag was raised above the city and the gates were locked to keep the people in until the ransom that had been agreed was paid.

The al-aqsa mosque, and the mihrab was a den of pigs and filth . . . occupied by all manner of   infidels   and criminals.

G The *Itinerarium Regis Ricardi* was put together in the 13th century by a monk. Historians think that it is one of the best sources for the Crusades of Richard I. Here the writer describes Saladin's capture of Jerusalem.

The citizens put up what barriers they could, but everything the people tried was unsuccessful. In vain they used bows, catapults and slings.

People from surrounding fortresses flocked into Jerusalem. But in that great   multitude   of men scarcely a dozen soldiers were to be found.

The terrified mob kept running to the rulers of the city. They asked for arrangements to be made to hand over the city to Saladin. For each person a ransom was paid: twelve sovereigns for a man and five for a woman, one for a child. Anyone who could not pay was taken captive.

H Portrait of Saladin drawn at the time. He was born in 1138 in Iraq. He seized power in Egypt in 1171. He is known to Muslims as the leader of Egypt, Syria and Palestine. To western historians he is known as the sultan who fought against Richard I.

The capture of Jerusalem was the signal for another Crusade. The Third Crusade was led by Richard I of England. He managed to recapture Acre, but was not able to capture Jerusalem. Saladin sat in the city and waited. By 1192, Richard was very ill and ready to give up. He had been abandoned by many of his followers. He signed a peace treaty with Saladin and left the Holy Land.

The Crusades continued for many years. However, the Muslim sultans were more worried about the Mongols – the travelling people from north-west China who were taking over the Muslim empire.

I Louis IX of France leaving on the Fourth Crusade for the Holy Land, 1203.

1 What do you think were the advantages and disadvantages of having a monk, Peter the Hermit, as leader of the People's Crusade? Explain your answer.

2 Sources C and D are written by Arab historians.
a) In what ways would you expect them to be different from a source written by a Christian?
b) Source E is written by a Christian. How does it differ from sources C and D?
c) Make two columns in your book. Put the heading *Invaders* at the top of one column and *Heroes* at the top of the second. Using the information on the Crusades, find as much evidence as you can which supports the claim that the Crusaders were heroes. Write this evidence under the Heroes column.
d) Now find as much evidence as you can to support the claim that the Crusaders were invaders. Write this under the Invaders column.

| 500 | 600 | 700 | 800 | 900 | 1000 | 1100 | 1200 | 1300 | 1400 | 1500 | 1600 |

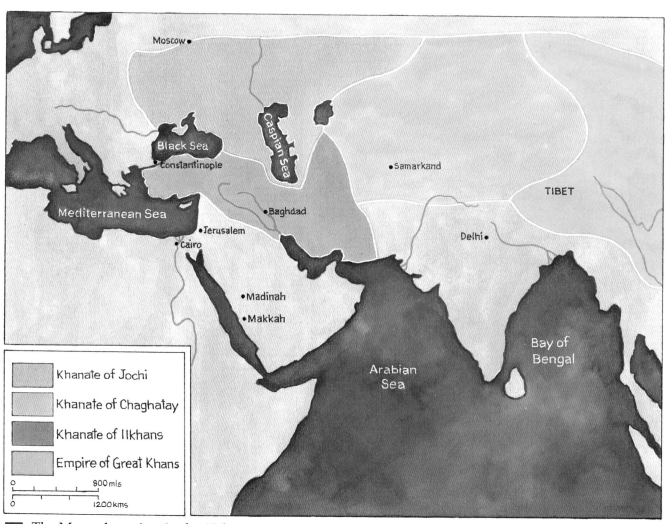

A The Mongol empires in the 13th century.

Whilst the Muslims were fighting against the Christians, Persia and Iraq were attacked from the East. In 1258, they were conquered by the Mongols from Eastern Asia. The Mongols were not Muslims. They were led by Chinggis Khan who had set out to conquer the whole known world.

The Mongols ruled over Persia and Iraq until their power weakened in 1336. Then many rival groups fought against each other. Eventually the land was taken over by a new Mongol ruler, Timur, also known as Tamerlane. He had been a sheepstealer, born near Samarkand in 1336. He gathered together a band of adventurers who attacked and defeated neighbouring chieftains and captured their lands. In 1366, he captured the city of Samarkand, which he made into his capital city. From here he moved into Persia, Iraq and India. He ruled from 1370-1405.

B In 1401, a Spanish nobleman visited Timur's court. He wrote about what he saw:
Timur was seated in the porch before the entrance to several fine   residences   . There was a platform on the floor, and in front of it a fountain which spurted water very high and in which there were some red apples. Timur was resting on small round cushions embroidered with silk, and was dressed in a plain silk robe. On his head he wore a tall white hat with a ruby, pearls and other precious stones on the top.

C Timur's court at Samarkand. This picture was drawn in the 16th century. It comes from a Persian book written about the life of Timur.

One result of Timur's attack on Persia and Iraq was to open the way for the Turks to settle on the frontier of the Byzantine empire. Nomads, bandits and refugees wanting to escape from Mongol rule came to settle here. One of these states, led by the Turk Uthman (Osman) I, later became very great. Osman set up a ruling family, the Ottomans, which was to last until 1924.

In 1398, the Ottomans began to plan to expand their kingdom. They aimed to take over Constantinople. Their plans suffered a set-back in 1402 when Timur attacked them. He did this because he thought they were getting too powerful. The Ottomans survived this attack and eventually in 1453, led by Sultan Mehmed, they captured Constantinople.

D Sultan Mehmed's biographer was a Greek called Kritovoulus. He praised the Sultan's good points and his kindness towards the Christians he had conquered. Here he describes how the Sultan rebuilt Constantinople.

He himself chose the best place in the middle of the city and ordered a mosque to be built there which would rival the biggest and the finest for height, beauty and size. For this purpose they were to collect the finest materials of all kinds . . .

The things people did in the past sometimes have immediate results. Sometimes it takes much longer for their actions to have any effect, and sometimes their actions have little effect at all. It is part of the historian's work to sort out the different kinds of historical change – rapid or gradual.

E This manuscript shows Turkish builders. It is taken from a Persian 15th-century manuscript.

1 a) Look at sources B and C. Say in what ways the written evidence agrees with what is drawn in the picture.
b) Do you think the writer and the artist saw the same event? Look carefully at the dates of each source. Gives reasons for your answers.
2 a) What were the results of the Mongol invasions?
b) Was there a connection between Timur's invasion and the capture of Constantinople? Give reasons for your answer.
3 How does source E compare with a modern building site? List the ways in which it is similar and the ways in which it is different.
4 Why do you think Sultan Mehmed wanted to rebuild Constantinople? Give as many reasons as you can.

A The Islamic empire at its largest extent.

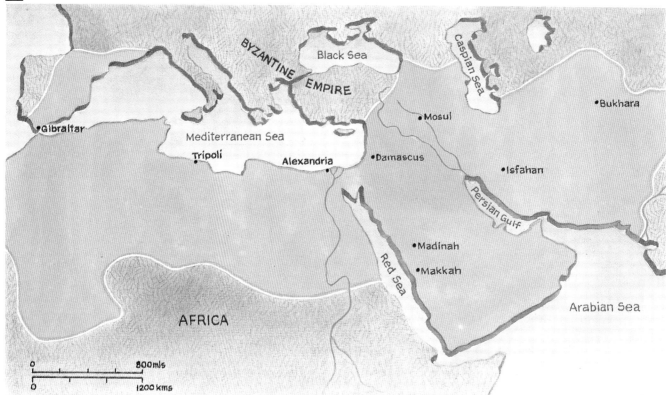

As you can see from the map above, the Islamic empire grew very large. By 642 Syria, Palestine and Egypt were conquered. This was followed in 661 by the rest of North Africa. From the stronghold of Syria and Palestine, Iraq, Persia and Afghanistan were taken over. North Africa was used as a base for the conquest of Spain. By 800 all these lands had been taken over by Islam.

Many reasons have been given for the development of Islam. Some of these reasons are personal, some religious, some economic and some military. These are some of the reasons which have been suggested:

* It was because Muhammad was a powerful leader.
* Muhammad was the last true prophet of God. It was God's will that Islam should grow.
* Muhammad wanted to carry the word of God to the rest of the known world.
* A belief in one God, Allah, brought people together and so helped to stop tribal warfare.
* Muslim merchants travelled far and wide to trade. They persuaded other people to become Muslims.

B Islamic troops riding camels into battle. Camels were very useful in battle because they could travel long distances without the need for drink.

- The Islamic empire got rid of frontiers and made travel much safer.
- The caliph had total power because he ruled as God's representative on earth. Any person who rebelled or challenged the caliph also rebelled and challenged Allah. No one wanted to disobey God.
- Islam made people more disciplined.
- Muslims allowed peoples who gave in peacefully the right to keep their lands as long as they paid their taxes.
- Arabic became the official language all over the Islamic empire.
- Jews and Christians were treated fairly.
- Muslims conquered other tribes because they were better fighters.
- Scholars were well respected. Islamic medical, scientific and geographic knowledge spread far and wide. This helped spread the religion of Islam.
- Arabia had very few resources. It did not provide enough food for its population. Many people moved north to Palestine and south-east to the River Euphrates.
- For more than two centuries there had been a conflict between the Christians living in Byzantium and the Christians in Europe. Neither realised how powerful Islam was at the beginning.
- The caliphs were strong rulers.

Historians want to find out why something happened. They do not believe that there is only one reason for an event. Different causes may be of various types. For instance, some causes may be religious, some economic, some political. For instance, a religious cause could be the rise of Islam. Sometimes all these causes are involved.

1 a) Please work in pairs. Draw this chart into your book.

military	economic	religious	political	individual

b) Using the pictures and the text, put each cause in the correct column.
c) Look back through this book and write a sentence supporting each of the reasons given for the development of Islam.
d) Write out these statements in the order you think is important.
e) As a class, compare your lists. Are they the same or different? Discuss why they differ.

2 a) Explain the role religion played in the growth of the Muslim empire.
b) Explain any other factors which caused the empire to grow.

C The King of Abyssinia receives Muslim visitors (1306).

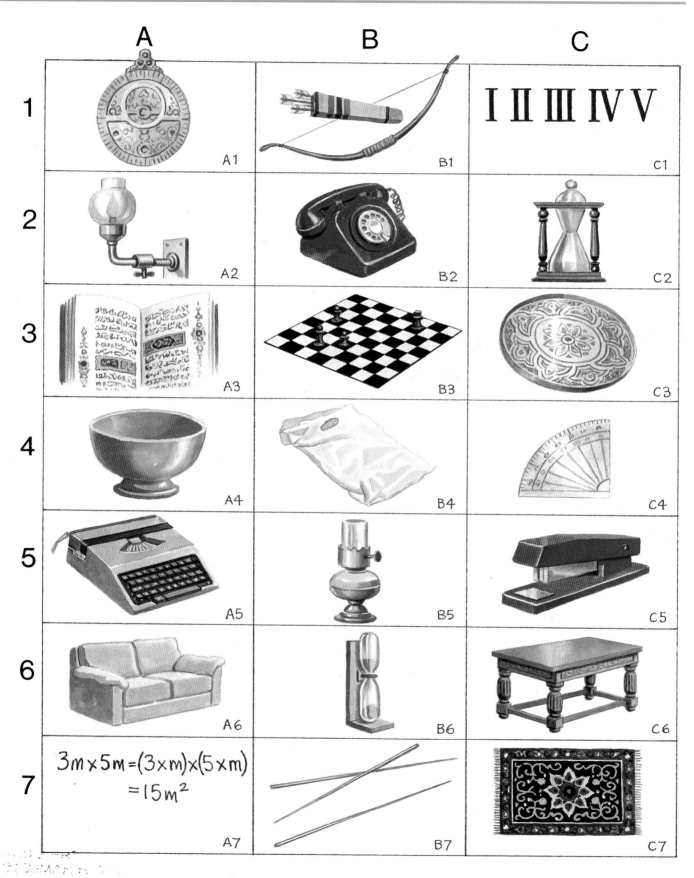

	A	B	C
1	A1	B1	I II III IV V — C1
2	A2	B2	C2
3	A3	B3	C3
4	A4	B4	C4
5	A5	B5	C5
6	A6	B6	C6
7	$3m \times 5m = (3 \times m) \times (5 \times m)$ $= 15m^2$ — A7	B7	C7

A Record Sheet A.

You can find out about the past in a number of ways. Books, written by historians, will give you information. You can also read what people wrote at the time, and look at their architecture, art and literature. Archaeologists look for items, called artefacts, that tell us what life was like long ago.

Archaeologists cannot dig up anywhere they wish. They usually look for the places where artefacts are likely to be found. They then dig long trenches to see what they can find. An accurate record is kept of exactly what they have found. A square grid plan is used to show where the artefact was found. Usually, the deeper they go, the older the artefact.

For this exercise, you are on an archaeological dig in Baghdad, searching for artefacts from medieval Islam. You discover many interesting artefacts. All the objects you have found are on Record Sheet A. Decide which objects you want to save and why. You will record this on your plan and evidence sheet.

We all live in a world in which everything changes so quickly. In the early part of this century people travelled on foot or on horseback. It took a long time to get anywhere. Now, if you wish, and can afford it, it is possible to travel by car, train, boat or aeroplane. America is only hours away.

Some things like travel have changed a lot. Other things have remained the same. People still play games like chess, eat from beautiful pottery dishes and use carpets.

Historians try to find out why some things have altered and others have remained the same.

1 Find out which objects on Record Sheet A are from medieval Islam. Use the rest of the book to help you decide. Draw these objects on a separate sheet of paper.

2 a) Copy out Record Sheet A without the artefacts in it. Label it Record Sheet B.
b) Stick the artefacts you have drawn onto Record Sheet B. Put them in the squares on the plan which match the code number of the object. Not all the squares will be used.

3 Draw Record Sheet C in your exercise book. Now fill it in. Use the rest of the book to help you.

4 Using Record Sheet C, write a few paragraphs saying why some things have changed and why others have remained the same.

Record Sheet C

Item number	What it is	What it was used for	Do we still use this artefact today?

B   An archaeological dig in Julfar, an Islamic harbour site in the United Arab Emirates.

GLOSSARY

abstract – art which is not pictorial

anaesthetics – drug used to make you unconscious before an operation

aqueducts – bridges with canals on the top used for carrying water

ascended – went up

astronomy – the study of the stars and planets

besieged – surrounded and attacked from all sides

brocade – rich cloth with a raised pattern

caesarian – a delivery of a baby by cutting into the mother's womb

chaotic – utter confusion

circumcision – cutting off a male's foreskin

civil war – a war between people living in the same country

congestion – too much blood or mucus concentrated in a part of the body

consumption – a disease which wastes away the body

contagious – a disease which is catching

Crusade – the name Christians used to describe a war against Muslims around Jerusalem. The word comes from *cross*

crystal – clear glass of good quality

discreetly – hidden away

dysentery – a stomach disease which is very unpleasant

economic – to do with money and wealth

emigration – movement from one country to another

falconers – people who look after falcons. These are birds of prey

grafting – a method used in growing fruit where the stem of the fruit tree is fastened on to the root of another tree

idols – objects worshipped like gods

imam – Muslim religious leader

incense – a slow-burning sweet-smelling substance used to perfume the air

infidels – people who do not believe in the same religion

inlaid – precious stone or wood cut into the surface of other precious stones or wood to make a pattern

irrigation – a system which allows water to be moved and stored in order to water land-growing crops

magistrate – a person who listens to all the evidence in court and comes to a decision as to what should happen

massacred – killed large numbers of people

muezzin – a person who calls the faithful to prayer

multitude – a large number

nobility – lords and ladies

observatory – a building from which stars and planets are studied

organic – without added chemicals

pagans – people who have more than one god or no gods

pilgrimage – a journey to a religious place

pious – holy

poll tax – head tax

prophets – religious people who interpret God's will

residences – rooms where people live

suq – a market

tanners – leather workers

tuberculosis – disease of the lungs

vessel – boat

worshippers – people who show devotion to a person

Zorastrians – followers of an ancient religion of Iran